A Yachtsman's Guide:

Smuggling Your Boat Out of Jail

The Foreign & State-to-State Maze of Cruising Regulations:
Avoiding the Snares & Traps.

Michael P. Maurice

Copyright 2007 by Michael P. Maurice

All rights reserved. No part of this book may be reproduced or utilized in any form or any means, electronic or mechanical, including photocopying and recording, or by information storage and retrieval systems, without written permission from the author.

Maurice, Michael P., 1946 –

Softcover Perfect Binding ISBN: 978–0–6151–8692–4

Coil Binding ISBN: not assigned

Hardcover Dust Jacket ISBN: not assigned

Hardcover Casewrap ISBN: not assigned

First Edition

To Order Copies: Contact the Author

<http://tinyurl.com/39lac6>

or

<http://www.yachtsdelivered.com/bookpub.html>

☎ +1-503-694-2221

Photo Credits

Cover: Dutch Harbor Alaska 2006

Back: Hakodate, Japan 2006

Page xii: Japan 2006

Kimley's: 2006

By the Author

Printed in the United States of America

Edit Date

4/28/2008 9:04 PM

Table of Contents

Photo Credits..............iii
Edit Date............................iii
TABLE OF CONTENTS.IV

FORWARD VIII

PREFACE........................IX
NON U.S. CITIZENS & BOATS...............................IX
CORRECTIONS TO THIS DOCUMENT X
ACCURACY........................XI
Report Errors..............xi
ADDED FOR COMPLETENESS XI
ACKNOWLEDGEMENTS XI
Technical Advice.......xi

SECTION 1 – ▷ INTRODUCTION 1
THE CAPTAIN'S AUTHORITY 2
UNIQUE COLREGS.........3
VARIABILITY IN LAWS, REGULATIONS & ENFORCEMENT 4
A HISTORY OF CLEARANCE LAW....................................4
LABEL MAKING..................4

SECTION 2 – ▶ CLEARING 5
CLEARING IN & OUT OF FOREIGN COUNTRIES.......5
Night Entry or Leaving 5

General........................ 5
U.S. Customs Web Page for Travel-by-Boat Issues.................. 6
U.S. Know Before You Go Web Pages........... 6
Health 6
Immigration.................. 7
Customs...................... 7
Agriculture................... 7
Clearing In................... 7
Clearing Out 7
Liquor........................... 7
Other rarely asked for Documents.................. 7
Garbage – Refuse 7
SECURED & SEALED IN A LOCKER. 7
CRUISING LICENSES-PERMITS 8
United States.............. 8
U.S. Reciprocal Cruising License Countries..................... 8
Other Countries.......... 9
EXEMPTION TO A FORMAL ENTRY................................ 9
ENTERING A FOREIGN BUILT BOAT 10
Vessel Never Before Entered....................... 10
YACHTS OVER 100 GROSS TONS............................. 11
COMMERCIAL VERSUS, RECREATIONAL................ 11
24(??) HOUR WARNING 11

Where to Find Notice
Times *11*
Australia..................... *12*
FINDING WEB SITES 12
Customs..................... *12*
General Searches on
Google *13*
Finding Cruisers
Information *13*
CREW ISSUES 13
RADIO LICENSES............. 14
Amateur Radio.......... *14*
CB RADIOS 15
HANDHELD VHF RADIOS 15
GUNS............................ 16
Mexico...................... *16*
BUOY SYSTEMS A & B ... 16
IALA BOUNDARIES 17
Maps......................... *17*
Atlantic *17*
Pacific....................... *17*
CARDINAL MARKS........... 17
DIRECTION LIGHTS.......... 18
SAILING DIRECTIONS 18

**SECTION 3 – ▶
OFFSHORE 19**

SHIP'S ID 19
ACCIDENT OFFSHORE,
COLLISION, ETC. 19
BEING APPROACHED AT
NIGHT............................20
SAFETY BOARDING BY
COAST GUARD 20
NEAR SHORE CRUISING
OBSTACLES....................21
EMERGENCY HELP..........21
U.S. Embassy or State
Department *21*

U.S. Coast Guard
Search & Rescue
centers...................... *22*
Piracy........................ *22*
IMB Piracy Reporting
Centre *22*
U.S. Citizens while in
Foreign Countries *22*
REGISTERING BEACONS. 22
EPIRB – 406 MHz ... *22*
Australia – AMSA..... *23*
EPIRB – 121.5 MHz . *23*
Search & Rescue
Insurance................... *23*
HIGH SEAS LAW.............. 23
Approached By
Another Vessel......... *23*
Tactics for Right of
Innocent Passage.... *24*

**SECTION 4 – ▶
CLEARING OUT.............. 27**

A SHORT... STORY 27
STAYING OUT OF JAIL......27
CHECKLIST FOR LEAVING
THE U.S. 27
Title or Document..... *27*
Clearance to Foreign
Port........................... *28*
Fly the Flag of Your
Country *28*
Extra Copies *28*
Ship's Stamp............. *28*
Local Currency.......... *28*
Credit Cards.............. *28*
Vessel Traffic Services
VTS *28*
EXPORT CONTROLLED
PRODUCTS......................29

v

SECTION 5 – ▷ TRAVEL DOCUMENTS 32

PASSPORTS 32
TRAVEL VISAS................. 32
   For U.S. Citizens...... 32
   For NON U.S. Citizens 32
   Visa Waiver Program (VWP) 33
ELECTRONIC TRAVEL AUTHORITY ETA............. 33
PARTS & MATERIALS FOR A VESSEL IN TRANSIT 33

SECTION 6 – ▷ STATE-TO-STATE 34

CRUISING STATE-TO-STATE 34
   Reciprocity Issues.... 34
   Live Aboard................ 35
   State Tax & Registration Issues.. 35
U.S. PILOTAGE REQUIREMENTS FOR FOREIGN FLAG YACHTS . 37
   Washington State Pilotage Waters........ 38
   Foreign Flag Yachts & Pilotage...................... 39

APPENDIX........................ 40

INTERNATIONAL DIALING 40
INTERNET RESOURCES... 41
   FCC Ship's License Help............................ 41
   List of Customs Web Sites 41
   Foreign Country Embassy's in U.S..... 42
   Embassies by Country 42
   Office of Naval Intelligence Piracy Reports....................... 42
   ICC Commercial Commerce Piracy Page............................ 42
   U.S. Internet Sources 42
   Reporting Suspicious Activity 43
   Establishing Residency 43
   Great Loop Cruising 43
   Canal Cruising Regulations................ 43
   Size information 43
   RYA European Waterways Regulations................ 43
   Foreign Cruising........ 43
   International Certificate of Competency.......... 44
   Seasickness 44
   Smuggling In the Old Days............................ 44
   Web Pages of Country Info 44
   USCG Regulations.. 44
   Light Lists.................. 44
   Notices to Mariners . 44
   Wiki – Notice to Mariners 45
   NGA Publications..... 45
   USCG CG–706 45
   Articles of Agreement 45
   U.S. Code Documents 45

Current Country Information 46
Shanghaiing 46
POWER OF ATTORNEY 46
TECHNICAL CONTACTS ... 46
FLIR 46
DEFINITIONS 47
Admiralty Law 47
Other Definitions 48
U.S. Code of Federal Regulations (CFR) ... 50
USCG National Vessel Documentation Center 50
Is the Vessel Tender Documented? 51
Boat Name 51
Numbered Vessels ... 52
Documented Vessels 53
Earthquakes 53
Tsunami 53
WORLD WIDE 54
Cruising Information. 54
Embassy Web Sites. 54
THE LANGUAGE OF SAILORS 59
U.S. STATE TAX ISSUES 59
Property Taxes 59
Definitions for State table 61
STATE BY STATE 62
Registration Offices . 62
Table of State Sales & Property Taxes for Boats 65
Coastal Boat Property Tax States 70

By Highest Sales Tax 71
INNOCENT PASSAGE – UN LAW OF THE SEA 75
Part II TERRITORIAL SEA AND CONTIGUOUS ZONE 75
TERRITORIAL, CONTIGUOUS & EEZ CLAIMS 81

BIBLIOGRAPHY 85
GENERAL 85
RECOMMENDED READING LIST 85
SMUGGLING IN THE OLD DAYS. 86

INDEX 88

FORTHCOMING BOOKS FROM CAPT. MIKE 90

SALVAGE 90
BOATUS SALVAGE 90
Salvage Form 91

Figure 1 – Bill & Stella Kimley. Hard at Work, Building Diesel Ducks at Zhuhai, China. "So that others may live."

Forward

PEOPLE who boat, be it inland waters or offshore, share an Adventurous Spirit, and value the freedom that is at the essence of being on the water. The goal of voyaging is to maximize boating pleasure and minimize boating hassles.

What Captain Mike has thoughtfully assembled is nothing less than a collection of precious gems. They are precious in that they have the ability to save our time, our money, preserve relationships, and to inform us of some very nasty and obscure marine regulations.

Even if we are experienced yachtsmen this compendium will serve to validate our understanding or may provoke some further investigation. No other marine resource covers the range of topics. From naming your tender, being boarded by the Coast Guard, and dealing with crew issues.

Captain Mike's advice comes from years of seafaring around the world on power and sailboats of all sizes and seaworthiness. As boaters we are aware that boating can change from the serene to the chaotic in an instant.

Although some sections and content may have less appeal than others, readers should familiarize themselves with the contents and the index so that specific chapters can be…

Referenced as needed… hopefully well in advance of any crisis.

As readers it is important to understand that a work of this type is never finished, but as an author there comes a time to get out the First Edition. As readers, this information has the potential to save a boat and crew. Thank you Captain Mike for sharing yourself and your knowledge.

Sally C. Hass
Pilot, "Spirit of Balto"
January 3, 2008

Preface

THIS book is for those who go to sea, cruise aboard small boats and hunger for some adventure, just short of being in more trouble than they can get out of.

This is not intended as a replacement for the usual cruising guides. It is simply a master book about clearance, foreign cruising, and state-to-state issues.

There are phone numbers and web site links. The long URL web site links have been supplemented with "tinyurl" links that will save you much typing and possible error prone entries.

This entire subject area is a kind of giant maze with dead ends in every direction. It is hard to find information, people to contact and get clarification, or to run down and eliminate rumors and erroneous information. This book is intended to help you put an end to such problems.

This material is oriented towards U.S. citizens, but I have included material that will be of help to citizens of other countries.

No one should completely depend on any of the information I have supplied here to stay out of trouble. Be especially wary of "jail house attorneys" that you meet in bars frequented by yachtsmen. The rumor mill is full of experts with a couple of year's experience who can get you into trouble. That is why I wrote this little book. If what you need to know is not here, it is time to consult someone who is a known expert in the field. I have consulted with such experts in its preparation and have taken precautions to prevent you from being misled.

There is a saying in yachting: *you are responsible for your vessel and crew.*

Non U.S. Citizens & Boats

The material is U.S. oriented, but I have included material and links that are specific to citizens of other countries. There is a complete list of embassy web sites[1] from which you can find the embassy for most countries, etc. At least 2/3 of the book is for you.

Where there is a reference to contact a U.S. Government agency, think **your** country's counterpart agency.

See Foreign Flag Yachts & Pilotage, also Cruising Licenses-Permits

---

[1] See page 54

Even where the information is U.S. specific, it will give you insight into what other countries are doing and with the web links you should be able to find the details that you need.

Important Note

The material contained here, defines what the technical, legal requirements are. Some experienced boaters will tell you that this material is nonsense. They may think so because they have never run into the problem and been fined. But, I can assure you that the legal issues have been carefully researched.

I have provided Internet links and references to the legal underpinnings where I could locate them. Where possible I have included tables which indicate how a group of jurisdictions treats some specific issue, like titling or whatever. Where such a table does not exist I have made an effort to note that fact.

Many of these technicalities are ignored or unenforced, which is why many boaters think *that it's not so*. I am not trying to give you advice, so much as information. What you do with it is up to you.

There is some information about Sales, Use, Excise[2], and Property[3] Taxes[4]. It is beyond the scope of this book to provide explicit information to you regarding such matters. I have included tables to help you find such details for your jurisdiction.

I have 50 years experience going to sea and have packed everything I know about this general topic into the material presented.

Corrections to this document

There are many URL links and as you may be aware they change from year to year and can easily become obsolete. I have no simple cure for this problem. However, corrections with working links can be found at this web page on my web site. If you find that a link is no longer working check the link below. If the there is no update link, send an email to alert me to the situation.

Can be found at:

<http://www.yachtsdelivered.com/bookpub.html>

---

[2] <http://tinyurl.com/yv4p6w>

[3] <http://tinyurl.com/2ckzc3>

[4] <http://tinyurl.com/23cz8o>

Accuracy

There is a lot of information packed into this book. There are bound to be errors, either from information that was originally faulty or from a mistake while typing or editing. I have taken precautions to assure that the information is accurate. Even then, it is only true at the time of its entry into the word processor. Regulations change and there is no substitute for the most recent info. The date and time that this document was last worked on is on page iii.

Web sites that present official information from the respective agency are the most accurate, followed by web sites prepared by secondary providers, followed by various web blogs and forums. Do not *bet the farm* on anything except official sites or information that can be confirmed from the official agency concerned. In the case of tax questions, you can get a rough idea from talking to other boaters, but the only safe course is to consult a tax expert, someone who works with boating tax law. Expert at your state's taxes, would be best.

Report Errors

In this document to the author at:

docerror@yachtsdelivered.com

Added for Completeness

Here and there I have included some bit of material not because it was very necessary but *for completeness*. In other words, someone may ask you sometime about some obscure topic and you will recall that I included it here, for completeness

Acknowledgements

Technical Advice

Duffy Bouvia, Dr. Bob Austin, Lloyd Billings (Unlimited Master, Ret.). Various contacts at U.S. Customs and U.S. Coast Guard.

Figure 2 – Japanese Navy Ship, Hokkaido Harbor, Japan

Figure 3 – Sunset on Japanese Fishing Boat, Kushiro City Dock

Section 1 – ▷ Introduction

Figure 4 – Curious Japanese Fishermen Meet Americans

AS you well know, you cannot *Smuggle Your Boat Out of Jail*, and that is the whole point. Since you can't, the trick is to not get it there in the first place.

I did not envision this as an *Encyclopedia of Foreign Clearance*. Think of it as *A Little Black Book* for yachtsmen where Foreign Clearance, High Seas Legal Issues, State-to-State Cruising, Taxes, Registration, Numbering, Handling Emergencies, Piracy and a myriad other little known topics can be found.

If you are reading this and think I am going to teach you how to smuggle, then you have been cheated! Which may well be your the first lesson in smuggling; it is cheating and you have become the cheatee (cheated), whereas, practicing smuggling would make you a cheater. I trust, you are taking notes, as there will be a quiz!

What I will not cheat you out of is a good read. Smuggling conjures up tales of Piracy, Rum Running, tales of the High Seas, and dark coves on stormy nights. I tell you how to handle various obscure emergencies involving the authorities, such as a collision or being arrested. Hard to find Info & Tips on clearing-in, or out of foreign countries.

First, a history of the word. The Old English appears to come from the German verb, *smeugan* (Old Norse *smjúga*) to "creep into a hole". Bootlegging is an American word associated with similar activities; it first appeared in the:

Omaha Herald in 1889:

> There is as much whisky consumed in Iowa now as there was before..."for medical purposes only," and on the bootleg plan.

A bootleg refers to the long leather boots worn by cowboys in the Old West. They were used to store all manner of illicit goods, including an extra gun, a bowie knife, or a flask of moonshine. Incidentally, a bootleg play in football refers to quarterback running pattern that entails making a sharp perpendicular turn around the tight end.

<http://ask.yahoo.com/20030>103.html

or

<http://tinyurl.com/35jvkv>

The Captain's Authority

The Captain's authority rests on tradition and Admiralty[5] Law. One of the most explicit, ignored elements of this chain of responsibility stems from Rule 2 of the COLREGS.[6]

> 2(a) Nothing in these Rules shall exonerate any vessel or the owner, master, or *crew* thereof, from the consequences of any neglect to comply with these Rules or of the neglect of any precaution which may be required by the ordinary practice of seaman, or by special circumstances of the case.

In summary, the Vessel is responsible to the Rules, the Owner is responsible to the Rules, the Master is responsible to the Owner and the Rules, and the Crew is responsible to the Master and to the Rules.

Note that crew can be held responsible for violations of the Rules. Violations by any of the parties can make them subject to civil penalties of up to $5,000 per violation.

The Captain's authority to enforce compliance with the Rules is obvious from the above. In short, the Captain's authority is absolute even in the presence of the owner. Lawful orders which emanate from the Captain's Discretion or Authority must be obeyed.

Failure to obey orders can result in the vessel being fined or detained, with those aboard being arrested and jailed. This is a real possibility in the case of an accident. The Captain is obligated to use force where necessary, to prevent an assault upon any person on board or to quell a mutiny.

The Authorities of the vessel's *flag country* have jurisdiction over the vessel while on the High Seas and *may be given* such jurisdiction for any acts which occur in a foreign country's jurisdiction.

---

[5] <http://www.admiraltylawguide.com/>

[6] <http://www.navcen.uscg.gov/mwv/navrules/navrules.htm>

Criminal violations which occur aboard a U.S. Flag vessel on the High Seas are subject to U.S. federal criminal statutes, with potentially significant fines and imprisonment; small craft are not exempt.

Unique COLREGS

Canada has the most comprehensive set of modifications to the COLREGS. Canadian Sailing Directions generally contain these modified regulations.

<http://www.tc.gc.ca/acts-regulations/GENERAL/C/CSA/regulations/010/csa014/csa14.html>

or

<http://tinyurl.com/bshm9>

A number of other countries with significant maritime activity have modified regulations for their internal waters. The U.S. Inland Rules are a specific example, but the U.S. is not an isolated case. You are subject to these rules which you may not be aware of when in the internal waters of some foreign country. Be sure to ask the locals as there is no table by country that I can refer you to.

See European Canals page 43.

Here is an example of the Canadian changes to the Safe Speed Section in Rule 6.

Safe Speed— Canadian Modifications

6(c) In the Canadian waters of a roadstead, harbour, river, lake or inland waterway, every vessel passing another vessel or work that includes a dredge, tow, grounded vessel or wreck shall proceed with caution at a speed that will not adversely affect the vessel or work being passed, and shall comply with any relevant instruction or direction contained in any Notice to Mariners or Notice to Shipping.

(d) For the purpose of paragraph (c), where it cannot be determined with certainty that a passing vessel will not adversely affect another vessel or work described in that paragraph, the passing vessel shall proceed with caution at the minimum speed at which she can be kept on her course.

(e) In the Canadian waters of a roadstead, harbour, river, lake or inland waterway, every vessel shall navigate with caution and shall comply with any relevant instruction or direction contained in any Notice to Mariners or Notice to Shipping where abnormal water levels, ice conditions or a casualty to a vessel or aid to navigation may

   (i) make navigation difficult or hazardous,

   (ii) cause damage to property, or

   (iii) block the navigational channel.

Variability in Laws, Regulations & Enforcement

Each country has unique issues with smuggling and the breaching of their security. For instance, in the Bahamas it is yachtsmen bringing small boats and motors and selling them to the locals, duty free; similar problems are also in Turkey. As a consequence, these two countries are very sensitive and have what appears to be irrational procedures; which are an attempt to prevent these transfers from occurring.

For instance, it is prudent to mark your tender-dinghy(s) with the name of the mother vessel, the state registration numbers, and have copies of the title and current registration.

There is a tremendous variation in the level of enforcement and interest shown by the local authorities. Where yachtsmen have abused the sensibilities and laws of some country like Turkey or the Bahamas the result has been stepped up enforcement. Keep that in mind when you visit foreign lands. You can spoil it for those who come after you.

A History of Clearance Law

The laws were not originally designed to deal with recreational vessels. However, in many places there is only one set of laws and recreational boats are subjected to them in an identical manner to that of large commercial vessels.

Label Making

Get a portable label maker, like one of the Brother[7] units or similar. Get plastic, not paper label material. Use it to mark critical ship's information. Without labeling, your vessel is essentially a "one man" boat, with which no one can properly assist you or take over, if necessary.

---

[7] Model PT-1280, $40.

Section 2 – ▶ Clearing

Clearing In & Out of Foreign Countries

Night Entry or Leaving

DO not ever enter or leave the country at night unless you have explicit permission to do so. In other words, be in radio contact with the authorities.

There is some temptation to avoid contact by radio where you do not speak the language very well. But night entries are likely to get you yelled at, or worse. Especially countries that do not get many yachts as visitors.

General

Keep the paper documents from all clearings. If done by telephone; be certain to enter the Clearance Number in your records, log book, etc. Get the clearance number or the name of your contact before your cell phone disconnects and you cannot find that person again.

Do not let anyone else talk to the clearance officer until you have that number. The fines for violating U.S. Customs Regulations are $5,000 per instance and almost any tiny mistake or lack of being able to prove the clearance can result in this penalty.

Record the Time, Date, Location and Clearance Number.

If you fail to hear the clearance number due to the conversation being prematurely terminated, call back and get one.

Especially with U.S. Customs, do not depend on anyone, not even an agent to finalize your clearance and get the number. One hour before arrival, make contact with them by phone or whatever and announce your intentions; where docking, what time, how many on board, nationalities, etc.

Where you intend to clear-in, you are well advised to have the phone number and be in contact during regular business hours with the Customs Office, before you get anywhere near U.S. territory. This may sound like being paranoid, but *things have changed*, recently. Try to be helpful.

The Customs people are just trying to do a difficult job and they need everyone's help. Point out that you bought this book and have read it and applied that which you have learned in order to be helpful.

This link leads to the reporting stations with telephone numbers for the entire U.S.

<http://www.cbp.gov/xp/cgov/travel/pleasure_boats/boats/pleasure_locations/>

or

<http://tinyurl.com/2vq3kr>

The Outlying Areas Reporting System (OARS); presently operates in the NE states and Great Lakes region, for details:

<http://www.cbp.gov/xp/cgov/travel/pleasure_boats/boats/oars.xml>

or

<http://tinyurl.com/35ga92>

If you cannot find a phone number to call try these:

Seattle WA area: ☎ +1-800-562-5943

San Diego area: ☎ +1-619-685-4304.

Portland ME area: ☎ +1-207-532-2131 ext. 255

Miami FL area: ☎ +1-800-432-1216 or +1-800-451-0393

U.S. Customs Web Page for Travel-by-Boat Issues

<http://www.cbp.gov/xp/cgov/travel/vaction/ready_set_go/sea_travel/material/>

or

<http://tinyurl.com/yovyb9>

U.S. Know Before You Go Web Pages

<http://www.cbp.gov/xp/cgov/travel/vacation/kbyg/>

or

<http://tinyurl.com/2lgggt>

Visa Waiver Program

Most of the world's air carriers can set up incoming travelers to receive a visa waiver good for 90 days upon arrival in the U.S. and many other countries. This waiver is not necessarily usable for other travel across nearby borders.

For instance, you arrive by air in Canada and get your waiver; then later ride on a boat from Victoria BC over to Friday Harbor WA for lunch. This is presently a problem. Phone the Customs Agency office at the destination before heading across the border thinking that your waiver is valid for such an excursion, see Travel Visas in the Appendix.

Health

Medical Clearance; sometimes a doctor, many times by one of the officials below.

Immigration

Handles issues regarding people, their nationalities, visas, etc.

Customs

Handles Duty on items you are importing: the boat, personnel or attempts to smuggle same.

Agriculture

Your food or produce.

Clearing In

Includes visits from Health, Immigration, Customs and Agriculture.

Clearing Out

Immigration, Customs, Port Captain.

Liquor

Many countries including the U.S. severally limit the amount of liquor that can be brought in with the boat and the duty on liquor is high.

Other rarely asked for Documents

Ship's Radio License, since you will be asked for your call sign and need to prove that it is legitimate

Vaccination Cards

Clearance From Last Port, see page 28.

Garbage – Refuse

Many countries are becoming sensitive about refuse. Here are a few guidelines.

- Separate your garbage into food, metal, paper, plastic.
- Do not contaminate the metal, paper or plastic with food.
- Do not use your electric garbage disposal near shore, inside three miles.

Secured & Sealed in a Locker.

In some countries Customs will allow you to place, in a locked compartment, articles like liquor, guns, cigarettes, etc. Seals will be applied and cannot be broken until after you clear their territory.

In the U.S. you will have to supply your own seals and a bond. Such a bond is called an International Carrier Bond. It is not clear that such a bond can be acquired for a yacht's operation, at a cost that makes sense.

If you have one of the combination locks with four wheels on

7

the bottom[8] that you can set the combination, by inserting a pin with the lock in the unlock state, then you could have the authorities reset the combination to a number known only to them. Have the number recorded in their paperwork. Your copy of the paperwork should not have the number, only the original papers should have the number; to be revealed only upon clearing out.

Later, you will only have to have them supply the number in order to remove the lock; no hacksaw required.

Cruising Licenses-Permits

United States

The U.S. Customs Service will issue Permits to Cruise U.S. Waters to a select group of reciprocating countries' flagged yachts.

Successive Cruising Permits

<http://www.cbp.gov/linkhandler/cgov/toolbox/legal/directives/3130-006.ctt/3130-006.txt>

or

<http://tinyurl.com/3322bo>

Cruising licenses exempt pleasure boats of certain countries from having to under go formal entry and clearance procedures (obtaining permits to proceed, as well as from the payment of entrance and clearance fees) at all but the first port of entry. These licenses can **be obtained from the U.S.** Customs and Border Protection Port Director at the first port of arrival in the United States. Normally issued for no more than a year, a cruising license has no bearing on the duty owed on a pleasure boat.

Under-policy, upon expiration of a vessel's cruising license, the vessel will not be issued another license until it again arrives in the United States from a foreign port or place and more than 15 days have elapsed since the vessel's previous cruising license expired. (Customs Directive 31-00-06, November 7, 1988).

Vessels of the following countries are eligible for cruising licenses (these countries extend the same privileges to American pleasure boats). This list is subject to change, most likely by additions.

U.S. Reciprocal Cruising License Countries

Argentina, Belgium, Finland, Honduras, Liberia, Sweden, Austria, Bermuda, France, Ire-

---

[8] Abus Marine Brass Combination Lock 15812, $21. <http://tinyurl.com/ynvg5h>

land, Netherlands, Switzerland, Australia, Canada, Germany, Italy, New Zealand, Turkey, Bahamas Islands, Denmark, Greece, Jamaica, Norway.

Great Britain, including Turks and Caicos Islands, St. Vincent (including the territorial waters of the Northern Grenadine Islands), the Cayman Islands, the British Virgin Islands, and the St. Christopher-Nevis-Anguilla Islands.

Countries by Map Area

Argentina, Bahamas Islands, Bermuda, Canada, Honduras, Jamaica, former British Colony Islands from above.

Austria, Belgium, Denmark, Great Britain, Greece, Finland, France, Germany, Ireland, Italy, Netherlands, Sweden, Switzerland, Turkey, Norway.

Australia, New Zealand

Liberia

A Horror Story

Read the story below of the yacht that got fined some $5,000 times 8 for not reporting in while on a Cruising License.

<http://www.the-triton.com/megayachtnews/index.php?news=827>

or

<http://tinyurl.com/325tfn>

Other Countries

The list of countries that extend Cruising Licenses to U.S. Flag vessels, see U.S. Reciprocal Cruising License Countries

Mexico does not issue a formal cruising license as in the U.S., but clearing from port to port is much simpler than in years past.

For other countries, consult local cruising guides for current information.

Exemption to a Formal Entry

An American owned pleasure boat arriving in the United States from a foreign port or place is not required to make formal entry (payment of entrance and clearance fees, etc.) provided the vessel is not engaged in trade; the vessel has not visited any hovering vessel. Is eligible if:

1) Any vessel that has visited a hovering vessel, if the master reports arrival as required by law and is in compliance with U.S. Customs and Border Protection navigation laws, and;

2) Any article on board by law to be entered or declared is reported to U.S. Customs and

Border Protection immediately upon arrival. If these requirements are not met, the vessel must make formal entry with U.S. Customs and Border Protection within 24 hours after arrival.

Provided that the vessel is American owned and American built. If foreign built and never having been formally entered, see Vessel Never Before Entered.

Hovering Vessel

19 USC 1401(k)[9] describes a hovering vessel as:

Any vessel that is found or kept off the coast of the United States within or without the Customs waters, if, from the vessel's history, conduct, character, or location, it is reasonable to believe that such vessel is being used or may be used to introduce, promote or facilitate the introduction or attempted introduction of merchandise into the United States in violation of U.S. laws.

Entering a Foreign Built Boat

If you are returning to your own country, boats built in another country are often subject to duty.

---

[9] See USC Documents page 45.

Even if there is no actual payment required, there is usually paperwork needed. In the case of a U.S. citizen bringing in a foreign built boat, even one that you recently took out of the country, Customs may require proof of the duty having been paid. Be sure you have a copy before you leave the U.S.

Dingy-tenders should have registration from your home state and be sure to carry a copy of the title with your ship's papers. There is a rumor that you can simply put the name of the mother vessel on the dingy and that is sufficient; such information is wrong.

You need proof of ownership for any separate equipment of any value and a $10,000 dingy is separate and substantial by any definition. In general, the dingy is exempt only if it has no motor or is used strictly to ferry the mother vessel's passengers to and from an adjacent pier or beach. At some level of value it should be registered and have numbers, regardless of its use; a proper dividing line might be $500 see page 51, Numbered Vessels.

Vessel Never Before Entered

In the case of an entry to the U.S. by a foreign built boat, if the boat has not ever been formally entered, then it will be necessary to do so. A special Customs form may be used in some cases but this form must be signed by the actual owner in person. Otherwise, it will be necessary to have a formal entry made by a bonded, licensed, customs broker. The difference in cost is about $500.

This process is required even where no duty is due. If you are bringing in a boat never having visited, be aware of this snare.

Yachts Over 100 Gross Tons

Any recreational boat over 100 GT is likely to be treated in a commercial class in some countries. There is no summary list for this issue.

Commercial Versus, Recreational

One of the things to keep in mind is that in countries or ports that are unfamiliar with recreational vessels, clearing-in and out is likely to be a hassle. As countries become accustomed to recreational boats they are streamlining procedures. But if you get to some country where clearing is still pretty awkward, try to be patient. Be sure to study the cruising guides beforehand for country or port specific information.

24(??) Hour Warning

Failure to provide warning of your approach to a new country or port is considered a serious issue in some countries. The larger the boat the more serious the fines or treatment. A few countries require more than 24 hours. Countries that are touchy about this include those **not c**ommonly visited by recreational vessels and those with security concerns. Check current info for the country involved.

If you provide notice by fax, radio, or whatever; be sure to get a confirmation in writing if possible. At least a confirmation number or identification (ID) from whomever you are in contact with.

Where to Find Notice Times

The Coast Pilots for the U.S. have some information. The Sailing Directions (NGA[10], U.S. versions) do not have the information in any consistent or reliable way.

In general it is hazardous to your pocketbook to rely on any but current information. Only current government web sites, email and phone calls can be relied upon.

---

[10] Formerly know as NIMA

Australia

Australia cost some cruiser about $15,000 dollars for not giving a *minimum* 96 hours warning, see the story at:

<http://tinyurl.com/ytta53>

The solution since they did not have a good communications system was to have faxed the Australian authorities before departing from their last port and getting a confirmation in writing, see 24(??) Hour Warning.

Australian Notice Requirements

96 hours notice may be given by either:

Sending an email to yachtreport@customs.gov.au

Sending a fax to ☏ +61-2-6275-6331

Phoning the Australian Customs National Communications Centre on ☏ +61-3-9244-8973.

You will need to provide the following information:

- The name of your craft;
- Your intended first port of arrival;
- Your estimated arrival time;
- Your last four ports;
- The details of people on board including name, date of birth, nationality and passport number;
- Details of any illness or disease recently encountered;
- If you have any animals on board;
- If you have any firearms on board.

Here is the URL to the Australian web page

<http://www.customs.gov.au/site/page.cfm?u=4791>

or

<http://tinyurl.com/2xz42j>

Finding Web Sites

Customs

Many other web sites can be accessed by changing the last two characters after .gov to something like "uk" for United Kingdom, etc.

There is another variation where the ".gov" is shortened to ".go"

.customs.go.jp, for Japan.

This web site has a set of links to about 60 of the world's major customs web sites. It is not complete and not all the links work and be warned, some of the sites are *not* government but private web sites.

World Customs Organization

<http://www.wcoomd.org/tariff/?v=3>

or

<http://tinyurl.com/2ktwqw>

Most of the sites have an English version. The key word "English" is generally near the top of the main page; just click on it and the page will refresh in English.

See Appendix page 40, a List of Customs Web Sites.

General Searches on Google

You can enter the string as a search in Google, for instance customs.gov.bm for Bermuda.

Adding the string "vessel arriving" may help to narrow the search down.

Finding Cruisers Information

Some of the web sites have easily found information for yachtsmen and some do not.

Crew Issues

You can get into bigger trouble over crew than you can imagine. A few rules of thumb:

1. Have crew whose passports are issued by the country you are about to enter.

2. If not #1 above, keep in mind that the boat and captain are legally responsible for each and every person brought into the country.

3. This responsibility is absolute and can result in the boat and crew being detained and fined.

4. In order to be removed from this responsibility, a crewman must be removed from the crew list by the proper authorities.

The boat is responsible for crew, their expenses, medical, passport, visa, and even their travel home, or being arrested.

You will not be allowed to leave the country without the same crew that you entered with, unless those crew have been officially removed from the crew list.

If a crewman wants to leave but not with you, they must be taken to immigration and have the crew list changed. Immigration will generally require that someone provide proof of how the leaving is going to occur; by plane, ship, (with a ticket as proof), or as crew on another yacht, etc.

If the crewman does not have the financial wherewithal to purchase a ticket out, you will be responsible. This can be a sticky situation as you may not want them aboard, but have trouble trying to get separated from them.

Be careful about taking a crewman on who may be some other boat's "castoff". The other boat may be desperate enough to get rid of someone that you will be misled about their true nature.

A checklist of things to verify about prospective crew.

- Verify the passport and its expiration date.
- Same thing for any needed visas
- Have it in writing that they are responsible for their expenses, medical, return home travel, visas and passport.

Radio Licenses

Technically speaking, you are required to have licenses for any transmitting equipment that you have with you, (Amateur/HAM, Ship's, etc). This is rarely enforced, but be prepared by asking other cruisers before you depart for the destination country.

Amateur Radio

You can always claim that even if, you have HAM gear and no license to operate in the visiting country, that you will not transmit without permission. Keep in mind that this may not be acceptable.

However, you can always point out that since you came by boat that you need the gear to transmit while on the High Seas. Whereas, those who come by land or even by air are in no position to do so and you are, and have such a need.

Foreign Country Operation

<http://www.arrl.org/FandES/field/regulations/io/#iarpcountries>

or

<http://tinyurl.com/25v3jy>

IARP Countries

Argentina, Brazil, Canada, El Salvador, Panama, Peru, Trinidad and Tobago, United States of America, Uruguay, and Venezuela.

CEPT

<http://www.erodocdb.dk/docs/implement_doc_adm.aspx?docid=1802>

or

<http://tinyurl.com/2y9uf4>

CB Radios

The non-standard use of radio equipment in foreign countries is almost beyond imagination. In some cases the authorities are concerned about the diversion of your equipment to rebel groups.

In many remote areas VHF marine band equipment is used by everyone for every purpose that you can imagine: taxis, police, travel services, grocery stores, hotels, and dive shops.

In some places where more economy of use is needed, the locals are using CB radios. You may very well encounter small boats using CB equipment and channels rather than VHF marine band equipment.

CB Channel 9 is generally considered the emergency channel. CB usage in Mexico without a license is reported to be legal.

In some Central American countries the local boats may be using CB and I cannot refer you to any definitive information.

If you have a SSB HF radio, most of them will receive at the frequencies that are used in CB, near 27 MHz.

<http://en.wikipedia.org/wiki/Citizens'_band_radio>

or

<http://tinyurl.com/34xx8j>

Handheld VHF Radios

In many parts of the world VHF Marine radios are used very haphazardly. These habits of use in some countries probably will not get you into trouble.

This is not the case in the U.S. where the *unlicensed* use of a VHF marine radio, handheld or otherwise while standing on the dock or beach is sufficient to get you a fine for $5,000.

The chances of getting fined are not high, but here is how to get one. Anyone who sees you doing it can report it. The FCC has listening posts around the country, they can pick up your transmissions.

If you get a notice of violation from the FCC, you are required to respond. If you lie when responding that is a felony; whereas the original violation is a simple misdemeanor.

Family Service Radios (FRS), are legal most countries, but not everywhere.

Guns

Now here is a controversial subject. In general, here are my guidelines.

There is almost no usage of a gun in a foreign country that you will be able to justify. So, don't think about it.

If the authorities do not take them for safekeeping, lock them up, yourself. Do not forget the ammunition.

See Storage Locker page 7.

If you have a concealed carry permit from your home, there is probably no harm in showing it to them.

Emphasis that you have one, not because you think it gives you a right to violate their laws, but because it demonstrates that you *are law abiding*. It is some proof that you are reliable or your home country would not have issued it to you. And secondly, that having it demonstrates your willingness to be law abiding.

After all, it is not a license to *DO* anything. It is only insurance against being arrested unnecessarily.

In the U.S. the misuse of a firearm by a concealed carry permit holder is so rare as to be considered an *endangered species*.

Mexico

Even in an emergency do not have guns or ammunition aboard, and enter Mexico without having written permission to do so. Call the U.S. State Department first, for assistance.

The problem is local officials wanting to confiscate your boat.

Buoy Systems A & B

IALA System B is used in the U.S., including Hawaii & the Pacific Trust; North, South & Central America, Bermuda, Philippines, Japan and South Korea.

IALA System A is used everywhere else. This includes the South Pacific, Taiwan and Greenland.

In the B System, Red buoys are kept to right on entering from sea. In the A System it is the opposite.

<http://en.wikipedia.org/wiki/Sea_mark>

or

<http://tinyurl.com/yqoo7b>

The IALA regulations do not specify the numbering system. In the U.S., Red buoys are *Even* numbers, and Green ones: *Odd*. However, Bermuda is part of Region B. Its Red marks are numbered Odd.

Here is a trick to help.

The Right Hand side when coming from sea, the day mark is always TRIANGULAR and the left hand side marks are SQUARE, regardless of color.

IALA Boundaries

Maps

<http://www.deck-officer.info/buoyage/ialamap.jpg>

or

<http://tinyurl.com/27yfnj>

<http://www.cgate.co.il/eng/Seamanship/buoy_lateral.htm>

or

<http://tinyurl.com/282m2v>

<http://www.nauticalissues.com/en/iala.html>

or

<http://tinyurl.com/2yczn5>

Atlantic

55 W, 55 N to 35 W

south to 5 N to 20 W

20 W to 65 S.

Pacific

80 N, down Dateline to 10 N

east to 120 W

120 W, south to 65 S.

Cardinal Marks

Used outside the U.S. in Region A especially where "returning from sea" is not obvious, and a Lateral Buoy-Mark would be ambiguous.

<http://en.wikipedia.org/wiki/Cardinal_mark>

or

<http://tinyurl.com/23m2hf>

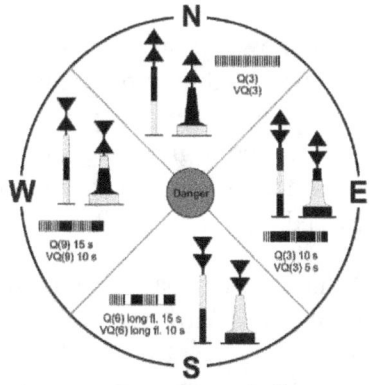

Figure 5 – Cardinal Marks[11]

---

[11] by Reinhard Kraasch

The coloring is Black and Yellow, which is not apparent from the picture above.

The safe water is in the indicated TRUE direction (not magnetic).

At night the cardinal mark flashes as follows:

North: continuously.

East: 3 times.

South: 6 times, plus a long flash.

West: 9 times.

Note, this is similar to a clock face: 3 o'clock for East, 6 o'clock for south, etc.

Direction Lights

A light showing white down the centerline, a red light over the location where a red buoy would be placed and a green light over the area that a green buoy would be placed.

Which means that the red will be on the starboard side when returning from sea in the IALA System B and green in the System A region, and so on.

Sailing Directions

Similar to the U.S. Coast Pilots, coverage is worldwide. Contain Navigation Regulation Information: details of obstacles, ports, anchorages, weather, currents, tides, fishing times and places, see NGA page 45.

Section 3 – ▶ Offshore

Ship's ID

BE sure to have your ship's Call Sign, Official Number, and Name on a label near the radio; that when queried you can provide quick and accurate ID. Remember you may not be the one at the radio when the authorities come calling or during an emergency.

Aircraft are the primary means of checking vessels within the EEZ out to 200 miles or beyond.

I would also have the Clearance Number posted near the radio. You may be asked for it. Use a small portable label maker, like the Brother units.

Change this clearance number label as you move from country to country.

Accident Offshore, Collision, etc.

Call the U.S. Coast Guard Rescue Center

U.S. West Coast, Alameda Calif

☎ +1-510-437-3701

U.S. East Coast. Portsmouth VA (Norfolk)

☎ +1-757-398-6231

as soon as possible. They can put you in touch with the U.S. State Department, if necessary. Do not be bashful, ask!

If the accident happened in International Waters, do not enter a coastal country's territory or waters without consulting U.S. authorities first. In some circumstances, it might be prudent to get out of the territorial waters. In which case you need expert advice. If the U.S. has a warship or other asset nearby they may come and help you. Even if U.S. authorities arrest you for some reason; in many cases it is better to be in their hands than some others.

If you require assistance and the situation turns into a Salvage Operation, be sure to consult the Salvage section in the Appendix, page 91 for the proper form. Tear it out of the back of the book if necessary; that is why it is in the back!

Better yet, print out a copy from BoatUS and fill in the blanks with your insurance company and phone number. Put this copy where you can find it easily.

Call your insurance agent as soon as possible.

Being Approached at Night

If you are concerned by another vessel coming around at night, especially if they are not lit; it will not hurt to transmit your identification (ID) on the VHF channel 16. Use 1 watt (not 25) and announce your ID with last port.

If they are dangerous and looking for trouble your transmission will put them off balance as they cannot be sure who else might hear the transmission or what other steps you might be taking. If they are a warship or security vessel, you will be simply starting the process and making it clear that you have nothing to hide.

Safety Boarding by Coast Guard

I suggest you prepare a one-page sheet with the following information. This is just a sample so change the information to match your situation. Notice that each item typically has the location for the item in question, as well as expiration date if applicable.

Hand this to the boarding officers on their arrival, who will be bowled over by your high level of organization.

S/V Invincible – #123456

Ship's Documents – Waterproof pouch (April 30, 2008), Plastic Box.

Preferred Mortgage – Ship's Document.

Most Recent C.G. boarding sheet – Ship's Document.

Oregon State Papers(123456) – Ship's Document. Sticker, Port Pilothouse

C.G. Aux. Inspection (2006), sticker on Port Pilothouse

Flares – With Ship's Document. Expire Nov. 2008.

Fire Extinguishers(5 – B1) – One forward cabin, 2 main cabin, 2 pilot house.

Life Jackets – Main Cabin (4).

Throwable Type IV Horseshoe & Cushion.

Oil, Garbage Placards – Inside of Outside Pilothouse Door.

Garbage Plan. With Ship's Document.

Rules of the Road – With Flares.

Horn – Forward Outside of Pilothouse Windows.

Head Located Forward Cabin. No Holding Tank. ElectroScan Unit.

Masthead Light – Front of Main Mast, 30 feet above deck.

Stern Light – On stern.

Red/Green Running Lights – Bow Pulpit.

Tri-Color Light – Top of Main Mast.

Bailing Bucket – Engine Bilge.

Bilge Pads – Forward Cabin.

Documentation Number – Welded in Hull, Main Cabin, forward end overhead hatch.

Ship's Name – On Stern, Bow.

Extra Flares – Parachutes, Smoke, Handheld – Main Cabin(not current).

Spare Air Horn – Pilothouse.

Boat's Documentation – Forward Cabin.

Bridge Clearance. 50 feet approx.

Near Shore Cruising Obstacles

Many of the world's coastlines especially those in what amounts to protected seas like the Sea of Japan are utilized for extensive fisheries. For instance, it is a bad idea to run within three miles of Japan, especially at night; as there are numerous traps, nets, and other obstacles.

In general the Sailing Directions[12] for the area will have notes concerning these obstacles. These notes cannot be completely relied upon.

Emergency Help

U.S. Embassy or State Department

The contact phone numbers here may not answer quickly. If you have a time sensitive emergency where seconds count; call the U.S. Coast Guard Search & Rescue numbers.

Consular duty personnel are available for emergency assistance 24 hours a day, 7 days a week at U.S. embassies, consulates, and consular agencies overseas, and in Washington, D.C.

To contact the Office of Overseas Citizens Services in the U.S. during business hours, call Mon–Fri:

0800–2000 EST

0300–1500 GMT

☎ +1-888-407-4747

or ☎ +1-202-647-5225 (after hours).

---

[12] See: NGA page 45

Contact information for U.S. embassies, consulates, and consular agencies overseas may be found at:

<http://www.state.gov/countries>

or

<http://tinyurl.com/36stpz>

U.S. Coast Guard Search & Rescue centers

U.S. West Coast Alameda Calif.

☎ +1-510-437-3701

U.S. East Coast. Portsmouth VA (Norfolk)

☎ +1-757-398-6231

Piracy

IMB Piracy Reporting Centre

Kuala Lumpur, Malaysia.

24 Hours Anti Piracy HELPLINE Telephone:

☎ +60-3-2031-0014

U.S. Citizens while in Foreign Countries

The U.S. State Department can assist you in ways that you can hardly imagine.

Arrange to get you access to your funds or help from friends or relatives, etc. Or, replace a stolen passport in as little as 24 hours.

If you think you might be arrested, contact U.S. authorities in advance and ask to have your situation passed to the State Department.

If you are arrested, immediately ask to speak to a consular officer at the nearest U.S. Embassy or Consulate. Under international agreements, the U.S. Government has a right to provide consular assistance to you upon your request. If your request to speak to your consul is turned down, keep asking—politely, but persistently. For information on how consuls assist American arrestees:

<http://travel.state.gov/travel/tips/emergencies/emergencies_1199.html>

or

<http://tinyurl.com/2sr5pm>

Registering Beacons

EPIRB – 406 MHz

An EPIRB should be registered with the country where the boat is from. Each unit contains a country code and only units with a U.S. code can be registered with NOAA.

https://beaconregistration.noaa.gov/rgdb/

or

<http://tinyurl.com/397u9j>

Australia – AMSA

For a beacon to be registered in Australia, all the following criteria must be met:

- The beacon must be coded with the Australian country code 503;
- The owner must be an Australian resident or company; and
- The primary nominated 24 hour contact should be in Australia.

If you meet the above criteria, get and fill out the registration form and send to AMSA by email, facsimile, or mail. Contact details are included on the registration form.

Residents of other countries buying beacons in Australia should have the beacon coded and registered with their country of residence.

<http://beacons.amsa.gov.au/Buying_and_registering/Registration.asp – top>

EPIRB – 121.5 MHz

Overhead satellites no longer pick up these EPIRBs but nearby search aircraft can.

Other SAR Centers

UK Falmouth Rescue
☎ +44-1326-317575

falmouthcoastguard@mcga.gov.uk

UK Beacon Registration

<http://www.mcga.gov.uk/c4mca/mcga-hmcg_rescue/mcga-hmcg-sar/epirb.htm>
or
<http://tinyurl.com/3bhx2c>

Search & Rescue Insurance

<http://www.geosalliance.com/index.html>
or
<http://tinyurl.com/38svbs>

High Seas Law

Approached By Another Vessel

RIGHT OF APPROACH AND VISIT

As a general principle, vessels in international waters are immune from the jurisdiction of any nation other than the flag nation. See Territorial, Contiguous & EEZ Claims Tables to determine if you are in International Waters, page 81.

However, under international law a warship, military aircraft, or other duly authorized ship, or aircraft may approach any vessel in international waters to verify its nationality. Unless the vessel encountered is itself a warship or government vessel of another nation, it may be stopped, boarded, and the ship's documents examined, provided there is reasonable grounds for suspecting that it is:

1. Engaged in piracy (see paragraph 3 S).
2. Engaged in the slave trade (see paragraph 3.6).
3. Engaged in unauthorized broadcasting (see paragraph 3.7).
4. Without nationality (see paragraphs 3.11.2.3 and 3.11.2.4).
5. Though flying a foreign flag, or refusing to show its flag, the vessel is, in reality, of the same nationality as the warship[13].

The procedure for ships exercising the right of approach and visit is similar to that used in exercising the belligerent right of visit and search during armed conflict described in paragraph 7.6.1. See Article 630.23, OPNAVINST 3120-.32B, and paragraph 2.9 of the Coast Guard's MLEM for further guidance.[14]

In summary, any nation's warships can approach to verify your identity. But, they may not board you except with cause as specified in items 1–5 or if granted by your vessel's flag country. If they attempt to board you are entitled know the reason. If you are alarmed, you would be within your rights to use your communications equipment to call for advice from your country's authorities such as the United States Coast Guard (USCG).

Tactics for Right of Innocent Passage

Avoid Anchoring if possible.

If you anticipate being forced to anchor, attempt to communicate with the destination state.

Give them fair warning from your last port of call, if possible. Such warning consists of the usual ship and persons on board information.

Get and supply a *Clean Bill of Health*, even a letter from the Port Captain stating the apparent health of you and your crew is useful.

---

[13] Fly the Flag of Your Country p.28

[14] COMDTPUB P5800.1

If forced to anchor

Advise that you will take the steps described below, "If forced to anchor."

- To advise the local state by best means: radio, email, etc.
- To not go ashore.
- To not allow anyone on board, not already on board.
- To not allow trading or physical contact with other vessels, or the locals.

Ask for provisional clearance to: anchor, go ashore, or take on fuel based on the information you have supplied. It may or may not be granted, but there is no harm in asking.

Emphasis that if such privileges are granted, that you will not abuse them, and if not granted that you will not violate the restrictions in any case.

Whether anchoring or not, to provide by radio, once a day (?) your location, course and speed, if so requested.

To provide these assurances in English, French, Spanish, German, or possibly some other language.

Some countries (states) are very picky about this and some not. Australia is very strict, French Polynesia is much less so, but this can change without much warning.

Archipelagic Countries

Antigua, the Bahamas, Cape Verde, Comoros, Grenada, Jamaica, Indonesia, Maldives, Philippines, Principe, Sao Tome, and Vanuatu.

Countries with Islands part of an Archipelagic group.

Fiji, New Guinea, Seychelles, Solomon Islands, and Tonga.

Table of Archipelagic States

See page 128

<http://tinyurl.com/36kwck>

Countries bordering Straits

Canada, U.S., Russia, Japan, Turkey, Spain, Gibraltar, Morocco, Malaysia, China, Taiwan, Turkey, Greece, England, France, Malaysia, Sumatra, India, and Sri Lanka.

<http://en.wikipedia.org/wiki/Strait>

or

<http://tinyurl.com/2tj2hd>

Major straits in the world:

- Bass Strait, lies between mainland Australia and Tasmania. Connects the Indian Ocean with the Pacific Ocean.
- Bering Strait between Alaska and Siberia. Connects the Pacific and Arctic Oceans.
- The Bosporus and the Dardanelles. Connects the Mediterranean and the Black Sea.
- Strait of Dover, between England and France. Connects the North Sea with the English Channel.
- Strait of Gibraltar, the only natural passage between the Atlantic Ocean and the Mediterranean Sea.
- Strait of Hormuz. Connects the Persian Gulf and the Oman Sea: Persian Gulf oil is shipped to the world.
- Strait of Magellan. Connects the Atlantic and Pacific Oceans north of Tierra del Fuego.
- Strait of Malacca, lies between the peninsula of Malaysia and the Island of Sumatra. Connects the Indian Ocean with the South China Sea. (One of the highest-volume shipping lanes in the world.)
- Palk strait, between India and Sri Lanka, the location of Ram Sethu
- Taiwan strait, between Mainland China and Taiwan

The trick in innocent transit is to make sure that you are transiting, not merely using a subterfuge to hide your intention to leisurely voyage from anchorage to anchorage.

Keep the following guidelines in mind:

Maintain a log, dates and times of anchorage, times on passage. An electronic log from your track log should be adequate. This assumes that you can demonstrate the time of each track entry.

Do not create the appearance of violating the customs of innocent passage. You may be over flown by an aircraft and photographed at any time.

Section 4 – ▶▶ Clearing Out

A Short... Story

How many times have I been approached by smugglers wanting me to smuggle their "stuff"? It is not that I have been approached personally, but what I do get are yachtsmen asking me if I have? As if, anyone in their right mind would trust me with a million dollars worth of pot to be smuggled!

Staying out of jail

It may seem redundant to point out that the easiest way to stay out of jail is to just play by the rules. Here are some tips on how to know the rules, which do change, and how to avoid some unintentional snares.

One reason the yachting community is so full of rumors is that none of the information is static and *things do change*. That said, most of this rumor information is in error in some respects. You need to know where to find the most recent sources for the information you need. This book is designed to help you do just that.

Checklist for Leaving the U.S.

Title or Document

If documented, original of ship's Document in hand.

If state registered, original of Registration and certified copy of Title.

Proof of Duty Paid, if foreign built. If proof not available, see page 10.

Boats which are not documented (state numbered), can be taken into Canada, Mexico, and other countries, but special precautions should be taken. For instance, a certified copy of the title would be a good idea.

If you expect to return to the U.S. within the calendar year, then purchase the U.S. Customs Decal[15] and put it up in the specified location.

<http://www.cbp.gov/xp/cgov/travel/pleasure_boats/user_fee/user_fee_decal.xml>

or

<http://tinyurl.com/l95wl>

---

[15] Private Vessel Decal (30 feet or more in length): $27.50 (U.S.) per calendar year

Clearance to Foreign Port

A *Vessel Entrance or Clearance Statement*, U.S. Customs Form 1300[16]. You will not need this going to Canada or Mexico, but there are plenty of other places that will require it.

<http://www.cbp.gov/xp/cgov/toolbox/forms/>

or

<http://tinyurl.com/m6qmr>

Fly the Flag of Your Country

This is not a mere formality, but very important as it is your declaration of your country of registration and can be seen by aircraft and other vessels. Consider it a matter of politeness[17].

Extra Copies

Hint, take many copies of certain of these documents when going international. Some countries want multiple copies of each document on every check-in and out of a port and it is a hassle to find a copier, and the prices for copies are sometimes exorbitant. Scan them into your laptop and use your own printer.

Ship's Stamp

Have a rubber stamp made up with the documentation number and vessel name.

A notary type metal seal is fancier and more expensive, but more impressive.

Local Currency

If possible, never enter a new foreign country without some local currency; if only enough to get you through the entry procedures that will allow you to go ashore.

Power of Attorney

See Appendix page 44.

<http://en.wikipedia.org/wiki/Power_of_attorney>

or

<http://tinyurl.com/2v669n>

Credit Cards

Inform your bank of your plans and obtain non-800 numbers to call.

Give someone you trust Power of Attorney just to handle credit card issues.

Vessel Traffic Services VTS

If you approach any of the major ports in the world, most of them have VTS. Which is not the same

---

[16] Formerly: form No. 1378.

[17] See: Approached By Another Vessel

as a "Traffic Lane" which the VTS most likely has several.

The edges of the Traffic Lanes are real important and you need to know exactly where the edges are.

There are places where there are Traffic Lanes, but no VTS such as in the waters north of Japan and east of Russia.

If you do not have detail charts you will have severe difficulty knowing where the traffic lane edges are.

The World VTS web site has "plans" which contain diagrams of the VTS area and the rough location of the Traffic Lanes.

<http://www.worldvtsguide.org/>

What you really need is the start and end points in GPS format, accurate to within 100 feet. This level of detail is difficult, but not impossible to get.

I put the start and end points of the edges in my GPS so I can see the edge of the lane as a line in my GPS on the chart-plotting page. This works even with a handheld GPS like the Garmin 76 units.

In the U.S., the edges of the lanes are defined in the Coast Pilots, see Chapter(s) 2, part 167.

Also in CFR 33 Title 167, see sample for NY:

<http://tinyurl.com/37adcm>

Strait of Juan De Fuca Lanes not in Part 167.

Export Controlled Products

If you have a Thermal Imager (FLIR) Night Scope, late model laptop, or desktop computers, or similar equipment; these items are subject to export restrictions. What follows is not definitive but in general:

Do not take such equipment to any of the embargoed countries, even if you keep the equipment and return with it; Cuba, Syria, North Korea, Libya, Sudan, and Iran are on the list of countries. Check the current list from the U.S. Departments of Commerce and State.

<http://www.pmddtc.state.gov/country.htm>

or

<http://tinyurl.com/2sur4z>

You may not require an export permit if the equipment is not taken to an embargoed country, or anyone on the lists of prohibited end users, or end uses. Such exceptions come under the NLR (No License Required). If you need an export permit, advice on how to go about it is beyond the scope of this book.

If the equipment is installed in the boat, and cannot be removed easily, and is an insignificant part of the boat's value; then it comes under the de minimis exemption (see page 47 Definitions). This does not mean that you can sell the boat with the equipment intact. In the case of FLIR equipment; contact them directly (see page 46 Contacts).

You might want to put plastic tape over the labels of components mounted on the outside that advertise the unique nature of the equipment; in order to decrease the chances of attracting unwanted attention to it. You can justify this on the grounds of security, potential theft, and vandalism.

Keep in mind that if you require any replacement parts for such equipment while you are out of the U.S.; you may have difficulty getting the parts or get into trouble by ordering them. Due to the variety of products that might be restricted it is not practical to describe all the possibilities. From a yachtsman's standpoint; the likely items are the one I mentioned above or possibly some computer software. Most anything that is restricted generally will have some warning label on the equipment, or in the manuals.

If you are asked by the authorities, make the following claims:

- That the out of country use is or was temporary.
- That no prohibited users or end uses have been allowed access.
- That you have *not* sold any restricted product, while outside the country.
- That you have not taken the product to an embargoed country.
- That your use comes under the NLR.

Do not lie about any of this. It is better to depend on their good sense that any mistake on your part was unintentional, than for them to find out you lied. They have ways of finding out about any lie that would take your breath away and it is not worth it.

In practice, the equipment that is really sensitive is the night vision equipment. Do not sell it or let any non-U.S. citizen use it or examine it. The penalties for these infractions are severe; most likely a major fine and jail time.

The U.S. Customs boarding officer is the most likely source

of trouble over restricted items. However, just because you get a pass from them does not mean a report will not be sent to some other government agency; with some action taken by one of them.

Unfortunately, the Customs people are likely to be unfamiliar enough with your particular equipment that they may feel compelled to contact one of the other agencies for guidance and you can get entangled in misunderstandings without any intent on their part.

If you have any sort of issue over such matters, make notes of: who you dealt with, the time, and place. Include their handling of the matter and keep copies of all documents you sign or they present to you for at least a few years. There should be no harm in showing them these guidelines and emphasizing that you have been following them to the best of your ability.

There is no statute of limitations in these cases or for that matter in regards to U.S. Customs. That means that whatever you have done is "laid in concrete" and proof and witness's can be brought to bear on you many years later.

Here is the URL to the Commerce Dept. web site:

<http://www.bis.doc.gov/licensing/exportingbasics.htm>

or

<http://tinyurl.com/33erka>

In summary, the most likely way to get into trouble would be to visit one of the embargoed countries or sell something like: a computer, or satellite telephones which have some restrictions. Check with your supplier.

Section 5 – ▶ Travel Documents

Passports

THE U.S. Government will allow a second passport to be issued concurrent with another valid one; if you have a travel problem where the visa sticker or stamps for say Israel, would prevent you from getting entry to certain countries which exclude tourists that have, or will visit Israel.

If you are going to use this two passport trick, be sure to keep the non-used one well out of sight when crossing a border where it could prove embarrassing. And, be prepared to explain it at crossings where you are not hiding it. Having two passports is sure to arouse questions.

Cruisers should insist on extra pages for their passport. This needs to be done at the time of original issue. If you do not have the extra pages, get it done at the first opportunity. You will need these pages if you visit many small countries one after the other, such as in the Caribbean.

Be sure to have extra passport photos, either for a passport renewal, replacement, or for Visa applications.

Travel Visas

A visa expires on its expiration date or the expiration of the passport, whichever comes first. Some countries do not designate a visa expiration date (Australia does this with business visas under their ETA program), in which case the visa expires with the passport's expiration. This fact could be useful to you. It might be worthwhile to renew your passport even if it is not within a year of more of expiration, country dependent.

For U.S. Citizens

<http://www.travisa.com/travelvisa.htm>

or

<http://tinyurl.com/2lb47x>

<http://www.visa4you.net/index.htm>

or

<http://tinyurl.com/2l3rg8>

For NON U.S. Citizens

<http://www.travisa.com/nonuscitizen.asp>

or

<http://tinyurl.com/2rvvqo>

Note: about half of all countries require a visa. From a cruiser's standpoint the ones that are the most troublesome are Australia, Brazil, and Indonesia.

You cannot get a visa or enter most countries if your passport is within six months of expiration. For U.S. Passport holders be sure you have enough room in the passport for the visa sticker; at least one page (as pages 22, 23, 24 cannot be used for visas). A passport that is filling up can have pages added but requires a trip to the passport office.

Visa Waiver Program (VWP)

<http://en.wikipedia.org/wiki/Visa_Waiver_Program>

or

<http://tinyurl.com/3bln5e>

Be aware that the VWP is not usable if you enter by sea or by air unless it is by a commercial carrier, and one that is a participant in the program. This eliminates yachtsmen, like us. I have included the information only for completeness.

Electronic Travel Authority ETA

<http://en.wikipedia.org/wiki/Electronic_Travel_Authority>

or

<http://tinyurl.com/35uyeo>

See Current Information page 46.

Parts & Materials for a Vessel In Transit

This is a very complicated topic and you need current information which is best gotten from local cruisers. Ask around.

Anything which can be sent by mail and marked "Vessel In Transit" accompanied with an "Invoice" on the outside of the package, has as good a chance of avoiding being held up by Customs.

The best way to get parts is to have someone hand-bring them to you. A copy of the ship's Document in their possession, and any other proof that will convince the authorities is a good idea; a letter from the vessels owner, etc.

Section 6 – ▶ State-to-State

Cruising State-to-State

Reciprocity Issues

DOCUMENTED vessels without a state registration in full force-and-effect must also obtain a **state** registration and display the validation decal on the vessel, when using some state's waters. Florida is one such state, posted on the Port Side. In Florida there is *NO grace period*.

This situation will only occur if your home state does not require registration[18] of documented vessels or you have been away long enough that you have not been renewing your registration.

Title, Register and Number all your dinghies.

Search for Current Info using
RECIPROCITY
NONRESIDENT VESSEL

In the Google Search Engine, add the state name if you want to narrow the search.

Searching under "RV" can be a useful topic for yachtsmen.

Documented or State Registered (numbered) Vessels

If staying more than a visited state's maximum (generally 60 days minimum), then register with the visited state's authority. Strictly construed this would include all the dinghies even those of foreign flag yachts. See definition, *State of Principle Use*, page 50.

There is no consistency concerning whether state numbering is only done in conjunction with issuance of a title.

The issue as whether you have to obtain a new title is unclear. Documented vessels are not going to be issued a title. For state registered vessels; in practical terms it may not be possible to obtain a title if you are not a resident of the state. This particular tiny issue cannot be determined except by consulting the administrator's of the state involved.

There is no published table of states that indicates what each state's policy is towards the issue of "short term" title transfers. State-by-state information is not available in table form.

---

[18] See: Phone Numbers, Reciprocity, Decals: page 62.

Cost of registration

Compendium of All U.S. States

U.S. Master Sales and Use Tax Guide. 2007. $85. CCH Tax Law Editors

<http://onlinestore.cch.com/default.asp?bu=fast&view=expand or >

<http://tinyurl.com/2qlfve>

U.S. Master Sales & Use Tax Guide

Online Copy of 2005 ed, at Google (not all pages online)

<http://books.google.com/books?id=gMqgJzEhFNcC&pg=PA1127&lpg=PA1127&dq=%22sales+tax%22+%22use+tax%22+boats&source=web&ots=OaaJ2fCXdY&sig=yx5XKtDsWKQxL123lCCG-jxxTO8#PPA9,M1>

or

<http://tinyurl.com/2978jw>

Live Aboard

Do not use the term: "Live-Aboard" when describing your status, when registering with marinas, insurance or governmental agencies or their agents.

State Tax & Registration Issues

Note that the information about taxes, etc. in this section is oriented towards visiting other states. It is incomplete in terms of the information you will need to address these issues in the state where you reside; although, the phone numbers and offices that you will need to contact are the same.

Definitions

Sales, a Tax on Transfers of Title except where exempted, one time.

Use, a Tax in Lieu of Sales Tax, one time.

Excise, generally some small amount of the vessel's worth like half of one percent, once a year.

Property, some states do not include boats in the property tax system; this tax is generally a local tax, once a year.

Registration, Titling & Numbering. The boat is subject to this, where "Principally Used"; not necessary until minimum 60 days (up to six months in some states). There are numerous exemptions, see page 62.

Marine Title has an excellent, but incomplete site

<http://www.marinetitle.com/index.htm>

or

<http://tinyurl.com/2nwvab>

Most states have sales or use taxes. Some have property taxes, a few have excise taxes.

The major problem with trying to produce a property tax table by state is that the tax is almost always a local jurisdiction tax, rather than a statewide tax.

The table on page 65 is correct in regards to boats. It is not applicable to property taxes on other kinds of property such as airplanes.

<http://www.boatus.com/gov/state_boat.asp>

or

<http://tinyurl.com/2jxr3q>

As far as registration is concerned the safest bet is to have registration from some state, whether you are documented or foreign flagged. It is not clear where that registration would best be done.

Detail state-by-state registration information

<http://www.dmv.org/boatregistration.php>

or

<http://tinyurl.com/3d7vov>

This is a summary listing of state numbering requirements for visiting boats. Period of time for reciprocity[19] and whether documented vessels required to be registered.

<http://www.boatus.com/gov/state_doc.asp>

or

<http://tinyurl.com/3bzb8q>

National Association of State Boating Law Administrators

Titling and Numbering

A book for $15,

<http://www.nasbla.org/references.php#Numbering>

or

<http://tinyurl.com/2k7v2f>

Summary of 50 State Boating Issues

Latest online edition is 2001, includes U.S. Territories, excellent reference.

<http://www.uscgboating.org/regulations/boating_laws.htm>

or

---

[19] See page 62

<http://tinyurl.com/2ktr7o>

Reference Guide to State Boating Laws; table 3–8 lists states requiring numbering, registration, or titling, penalties in table 3–7.

State Decals lost, damaged or removed for maintenance can generally be replaced for a small fee, contact your state of issuance.

Internet Discussions of Tax Issues

Florida seems to have the best web presence of any state and I have included links to their material; the pages are quite educational.

Florida:

<http://www.cruisersnet.net/index.php?categoryid=42>

<http://tinyurl.com/2r4k3l>

or

<http://www.irbs.com/lists/trawlerworld/9906/0560.html >

or

<http://tinyurl.com/3c8p4p>

Florida State Web Pages

Sales and Use Taxes

<http://dor.myflorida.com/dor/taxes/sut_boat_owner.html>

or

<http://tinyurl.com/3y3cqx>

Vessel Registration, Titles, Numbering

<http://www.hsmv.state.fl.us/dmv/vslfacts.html#1>

or

<http://tinyurl.com/2qjca8>

Florida has a Sojourners Permit form HSMV 87244 for use by out-of-state residents who need registration when staying beyond 90 days.

U.S. Documentation Issues

Pacific Maritime Title

Molly Holden, Manager
655 NE Northlake Way
Seattle, WA 98105
Tel: ☎ +1-206-632-4668

Fax: ☎ +1-206-632-4673

U.S. Pilotage Requirements for Foreign Flag Yachts

In general the U.S. Coast Pilots state that *All Foreign Flag Vessels* require a pilot. The Coast Pilot No. 7 for 1957 says *all vessels*. It appears that sometime since 1957 the Coast Pilots have been changed to exclude *U.S. Flag* Yachts.

This business of requiring a pilot aboard for foreign flag yachts has never been enforced, except perhaps very haphazardly. As it obviously was never enforced for domestically flagged yachts in years past.

Some places on the U.S. East Coast only require a pilot for vessels with more than 9 foot of draft.

Alaska and Washington have special rules for foreign flag yachts; other states may have as well. Consult the Coast Pilot for each state under the heading *Pilotage*. It will be found near the beginning of the section for the state of interest. See the State of Washington, page 38.

The argument for requiring a pilot is that safety is involved. The counter argument is that today's yachts are so much safer than in the past, with GPS, electronic chart plotting, and radar; that the size of vessel that justifies a licensed pilot should not include most yachts, regardless of flag.

Washington State Pilotage Waters

All foreign flag yachts, (except Canadian[20]) require a licensed pilot to be aboard. Exemptions are granted to certain vessels below 200 feet. The fee for an exemption starts at US$300.

Pilotage, Strait of Juan de Fuca and Puget Sound

(79) Pilotage is compulsory for all foreign vessels and - U.S. vessels engaged in foreign trade. Pilotage is optional for U.S. vessels engaged in the coastwise trade – with a federally licensed pilot on board. (Coast Pilot No. 7, 2007ed.)

Pilotage waters are those east of Port Angeles and includes the San Juan Islands.

WAC 363–116–360 Exempt vessels

(1) Under the authority of RCW 88.16.070, application may be made to the board of pilotage commissioners to seek exemption from the pilotage requirements for the operation of a limited class of small passenger vessels or yachts, which are not more than five hundred gross tons (international), do not exceed two hundred feet in length, and are operated exclusively in the waters of the Puget Sound pilotage district and lower British Columbia. For purposes of this section, any vessel carrying passengers for a fee, including yachts under charter where both the vessel and crew are provided for a fee, shall be considered a passenger vessel.

---

[20] Can't confirm about Canadian.

Foreign Flag Yachts & Pilotage

Since the requirement for a pilot has historically been unenforced, you can make a case that enforcement against your vessel is discriminatory. First on the basis that there is no credible difference in safety between domestic and foreign yachts, and secondly that it was unnecessary for domestic yachts, even at the time that it was required back in the 1950's.

Unless you want to make a court case out of it, you may not get very far with this argument, but it is a valid argument. In the meantime, if you do not want to be singled out, the only steps you can take are to keep a low profile. Do not fly your foreign flag and stay out of the commercial traffic areas where you may be noticed.

There is one other possible line of attack if you intend to cruise in the U.S. for a year or more, and that is to have the boat State Registered & Numbered in the U.S. If you do that, you avoid all the Customs Cruising License issues: clearing, reporting, and the state pilotage problems. (Note: you cannot document a boat in the U.S. unless the owner is a U.S. citizen. In which case if the ownership is wholly by U.S. citizens then you could transfer the registration from foreign to U.S. and back later if you wanted).

If you register the boat U.S., then you will be subject to U.S. Coast Guard inspections and will have to have life jackets and other equipment with USCG approvals. The expense of a few life jackets and a life ring may be a small price to pay to avoid all these other hassles. However, there is one major issue left and that is duty on the boat. If it was built outside the U.S. then it may be subject to duty.

Appendix

International Dialing

DIALING across the international phone system can be tricky. Be sure to test your dialing access to a test number using the same dialing access that would be needed for any of the emergency numbers that I have included.

It is assumed that any phone number you call that came from this book is being dialed from a satellite phone or from outside the country where the number is located. The dialing codes have the format where the leading "+" is the access to international dialing. The digits that immediately follow are those of the "country code", followed by the so-called "local number".

For instance:

+1-202-123-1234 is a number for the U.S.; country code is "1", the area code is 202 and the local number is 123-1234. Such a number would be in Washington DC.

The international dialing prefix is generally 011, or 001 and depends upon where you are dialing from. In the case of an Iridium satellite phone, the "+" button can be pressed and held until the "+" is visible in the screen. Then the country code and local number can be entered. This simplifies the procedure.

The example above would be 011-1-202-123-1234, from the Iridium, if not using the special "+" key.

Here is a URL that provides online-lookup, dialing instructions by country:

<http://www.countrycallingcodes.com/>

or

<http://tinyurl.com/2oufa>

For instance, dialing from UK to the U.S. the international access code is 00. Whereas, from the U.S. to the UK it is 011; then followed by the country code and number.

Here are the WIKI country code information pages with many links to more detail.

<http://en.wikipedia.org/wiki/List_of_country_calling_codes>

or

<http://tinyurl.com/joxfw>

You may see numbers provided by others who did not understand the International Access Code and they may have confused the situation by adding what they thought was the access code. When in fact, depending upon the called-from country, the code may be one of the ones I mentioned above or it might be something else entirely.

For instance, "Transiting the Panama Canal" by David Wilson gave a phone number of 011-507-223-4146. The actual number is +507-223-4146. He assumed that the access code was 011 plus the number, but that is not correct (4146 is a frequency number for a SSB channel just above 4.125 MHz). The access code would be whatever it is in the country you are calling from, like 00 or 011 or ??.

Another confusion can come about where I was given a Mexican number like this:

044-624-999-1234

But it can only be dialed this way from a Mexican phone, most likely a landline. In order to dial from the U.S., Iridium, etc. the coding is:

+52-624-999-1234 or

011-52-xxx-xxx-xxxx.

However, there is one more wrinkle. The actual phone I was calling was a cell phone and such a phone requires an additional "1" after the 52 country code, like this:

+52-1-624-999-1234.

You will run into many similar combinations. I do not have a complete set of rules to help stop this confusion, but this site should give you the answer

<http://www.kropla.com/dialcode.htm>

or

<http://tinyurl.com/mm5nb>

Internet Resources

If a link no longer works, try removing the text after the web site definition so that you will be taken to the main page; since the specific page may have been deleted or renamed.

Note: some of the web links failed to work properly; I have inserted a *tinyurl* link that generally works and have left the original in case you have to enter the string by hand. Tinyurl.com is a web site that converts long URL strings into short ones.

FCC Ship's License Help

<http://www.shiplicense.com/>

List of Customs Web Sites

A general list of 67 countries

<http://www.aduanaargentina.com/listado_en.php?seccion=24>

By Country

Argentina

<http://www.aduanaargentina.com/listado_en.php?seccion=30>

Australia

<http://www.customs.gov.au/site/page.cfm?u=4260>

<http://www.customs.gov.au/site/page.cfm?u=4791 >

or

<http://tinyurl.com/2xz42j>

Bermuda	.customs.gov.bm
Chile	.aduana.cl
Canada	.cbsa.gc.ca
China	.customs.gov.cn
Cuba	.aduana.cu
Hong Kong	.customs.gov.hk
Indonesia	.beacukai.go.id
Japan	.customs.go.jp
Maldives	.customs.gov.mv

New Zealand   .customs.govt.nz

New Guinea   .customs.gov.pg/yachts.html

S. Korea	.customs.go.kr
Singapore	.customs.gov.sg
S. Africa	.sars.gov.za
Thailand	.customs go.th
Turkey	gumruk.gov.tr
UK	customs.hmrc.gov.uk

Foreign Country Embassy's in U.S.

<http://www.state.gov/s/cpr/rls/dpl/32122.htm >

or

<http://tinyurl.com/3cs6gc>

Embassies by Country

<http://www.embassyworld.com/ >

or

<http://tinyurl.com/32xp78>

Office of Naval Intelligence Piracy Reports

<http://pollux.nss.nima.mil/onit/onit_j_main.html >

or

<http://tinyurl.com/2lwyf6>

ICC Commercial Commerce Piracy Page

<http://www.iccccs.org/prc/piracyreport.php >

or

<http://tinyurl.com/9sztl>

U.S. Internet Sources

Embassies, Consuls

<http://usembassy.state.gov/ >

or

<http://tinyurl.com/heqpn>

State Department Notes, by Country
<http://www.state.gov/r/pa/ei/bgn/>

or

<http://tinyurl.com/4srq5>

Pleasure Boats
<http://www.cbp.gov/xp/cgov/travel/pleasure_boats/>

or

<http://tinyurl.com/2wzpq6>

<http://www.drugstory.org/drug_traffic/smuggling.asp>

or

<http://tinyurl.com/32fblp>

Reporting Suspicious Activity

U.S. Customs.
☏ +1-800-BE-ALERT, security or actual smuggling.

Establishing Residency
<http://hubpages.com/hub/state-residency>

or

<http://tinyurl.com/2pocwe>

Great Loop Cruising
<http://en.wikipedia.org/wiki/Great_loop>

or

<http://tinyurl.com/35n9qr>

Canal Cruising Regulations
<http://www.canals.com/>

<http://www.bargingineurope.com/licensing.htm>

or

<http://tinyurl.com/3dnnuy>

Size information

<http://www.canals.com/size.htm>

or

<http://tinyurl.com/39y5lm>

RYA European Waterways Regulations

The CEVNI Rules Explained

<http://www.amazon.co.uk/RYA-European-Waterways-Regulations-Explained/dp/0954730100>

or

<http://tinyurl.com/2nyorg>

There is also a Waterways Manual; a cruising guide.

Adlard Coles Inland Waterways.

Foreign Cruising

Vol. 1: Atlantic Coast of Europe & Baltic Sea

Vol. 2: Mediterranean and the Black Sea

International Certificate of Competency

<http://www.rya.org.uk/KnowledgeBase/boatingabroad/icc/>

or

<http://tinyurl.com/2qude8>

Seasickness

<http://curingseasickness.com>

Smuggling In the Old Days

Britain

<http://www.smuggling.co.uk/buybook.html >

or

<http://tinyurl.com/3d2g74>

Web Pages of Country Info

<http://www.noonsite.com/Countries>

USCG Regulations

Marine Safety Manual

 * Volume 1 – Administration And Management

 * Volume 2 – Materiel Inspection

 * Volume 3 – Marine Personnel

 * Volume 4 – Technical

 * Volume 5 – Investigations

 * Volume 6 – Ports and Waterways Activities

 * Volume 9 – Environmental Protection

<http://www.uscg.mil/hq/g%2Dm/nmc/pubs/msm/>

or

<http://tinyurl.com/355gq6>

Light Lists

USCG

<http://www.navcen.uscg.gov/pubs/LightLists/LightLists.htm>

or

<http://tinyurl.com/yvcbw6>

Notices to Mariners

USCG – Local Notices

<http://www.navcen.uscg.gov/lnm/>

or

<http://tinyurl.com/3ykwu7>

NGA – Notices

<http://www.nga.mil/portal/site/maritime/?epi_menuItemID=2fbece2b0f5de897dc3f8c107d27a759&epi_menuID=e106a3b5e50edce1fec24fd73927a759&epi_baseMenuID=e106a3b5e50edce1fec24fd73927a759>

or

<http://tinyurl.com/3xk8jb>

British Admiralty

<http://www.ukho.gov.uk/amd/noticeToMariners.asp>

or

<http://tinyurl.com/2wadbp>

Australia

<http://www.hydro.gov.au/n2m/notices.htm>

or

<http://tinyurl.com/33lzgx>

New Zealand

<http://www.hydro.linz.govt.nz/ntm/index.asp>

or

<http://tinyurl.com/2uxnt9>

Various other Governments, and local jurisdictions.

Too extensive to list here. Search Google, "notice to mariners", then, add a country or local jurisdiction name.

Wiki – Notice to Mariners

<http://en.wikipedia.org/wiki/Notice_to_Mariners>

or

<http://tinyurl.com/2wxcc3>

NGA Publications

<http://tinyurl.com/lh2nr>

Mariners Handbook (NP100), British Admiralty, Extracts from Navigation Regs.

<http://tinyurl.com/yonyft>

USCG CG–706

Official Logbook, PDF

<http://www.uscg.mil/hq/gm/marpers/logbook.pdf>

or

<http://tinyurl.com/2hshn6>

Articles of Agreement

CG–705

<http://tinyurl.com/24mlln>

U.S. Code Documents

<http://www.gpoaccess.gov/uscode/index.html>

or

<http://tinyurl.com/2ezshe>

There is a relation between USC documents and CFR documents. If you have a reference that is in USC format then you will have to search in that part of the GPO.

For instance, go to the links provided above and to find "19 USC 1401k", enter in the search window, "19USC1401", leave out the quotes.

Current Country Information

U.S. Department of State Consular Sheets, by Country

<http://travel.state.gov/travel/cis_pa_tw/cis/cis_1765.html>

or

<http://tinyurl.com/4ow7g>

Shanghaiing

<http://wapedia.mobi/en/Shanghai_(verb)>

or

<http://tinyurl.com/ywn65q>

Power of Attorney

You need a power of attorney form to provide the authority for someone to take charge of the boat in case the Captain of Record is incapacitated or dies.

Limited Power of Attorney

To whom it may concern:

I, xxxxxx, owner of the vessel xxxxx, USA(or whatever) registration number, (include the HIN if available), do authorize that in the event of my death, incapacitation due to illness or injury, or absence that the following herein named individual, (xxxxx name), be empowered with all the authority of Captain of Record for any purpose that may be necessary for the vessel. Specifically to operate or sail said vessel, make arrangements for trans-shipment, storage or to hire another Captain to perform the same.

The individual authorized above, shall be authorized to sign legal documents necessary for the vessel's operation or to carry out this power of attorney.

Signed this xxxx day of xxxx 200x

Signature

Witnessed by:

Xxxxx, xxxx

Notarized by

Xxxxxx

You will also need a power of attorney for someone to handle some of your affairs back home.

Warning, the Power of Attorney may not be recognized if the person who authorized it is dead.

Technical Contacts

FLIR

Their Export expert is Melissa Wilkinson. ☎ +1-805-690-7176, the ECCN number for the

Mariner model is 6A003, section B4.

Definitions

Admiralty Law

<http://en.wikipedia.org/wiki/Admiralty_law>

Admiralty Law comes to us from maritime traditions formulated by Roman and Byzantine compacts and later by the Hanseatic League, a trade guild whose influence extended from the Baltic to the North Sea during the 13–17th centuries.

When Eleanoire of Aquitaine, mother of Richard the Lionheart returned from The Crusades with her first husband the French King, she introduced Admiralty Law into her realm and later into England when she was regent for her son. (See the film *The Lion in Winter*).

Admiralty Law is not based on English Common Law but stems from the Corpus Juris Civilis of the Emperor Justinian. Admiralty courts are civil courts with a judge but no jury.

Law of the Sea (LOTS)

<http://www.globelaw.com/LawSea/ls82_1.htm >

or

<http://tinyurl.com/2s998l>

Foreign Country

The land territory, and the adjacent territorial sea[21].

Innocent Passage, Right of

See LOTS, Part 2, Sec. 3. page 64. As of 2003 there were 157 signatories and 143 ratifications of the Law of the Sea.

For instance, in the case of U.S. and Canadian boaters, there are times where you cross back and forth over the boundary. So long as you do not tie up, anchor, or come into physical contact with a vessel that has yet to clear U.S. or Canadian customs, you are not in violation of any law or regulation. Innocent Passage has obligations as well as a Right: no threat to the nearby country, use of or practicing with arms, or spreading propaganda, etc.

Innocent Passage allows one to "pass through" Canadian or other foreign waters.

Territorial Sea

No more than 12 nautical miles.

See tables, page 81.

Contiguous Zone

---

[21] Territorial, Contiguous & EEZ Claims page 81.

Generally, no more than 24 miles within which a state can exert limited control for the purpose of preventing or punishing: infringement of its customs, fiscal, immigration or sanitary laws and regulations within its territory or territorial sea.

The U.S. zone is 24 miles.

Tables by country, Territorial Sea, Contiguous Zone and EEZ.

<http://en.wikipedia.org/wiki/Territorial_waters>

or

<http://tinyurl.com/2pxp3d>

See also tables page 81.

Hindering Innocent Passage

See LOTS. Sec. 3, Articles 22, 23, 24, 25, 26, see page 64.

Innocent Passage

A concept in Admiralty Law, also defined in the Law of the Sea (LOTS), which allows for a vessel to pass through the territorial waters of another state subject to certain restrictions.

The U.S. Dept. of Defense defines innocent passage as:

> The right of all ships to engage in continuous and expeditious surface passage through the territorial sea and Archipelagic waters of foreign coastal states in a manner not prejudicial to its peace, good order, or security.
>
> Passage includes stopping and anchoring, but only if incidental to ordinary navigation or necessary by force majeure or distress, or for the purpose of rendering assistance to persons, ships, or aircraft in danger or distress.

There is some difference between the UN definitions and the U.S. Dept. of Defense.

Anchoring is a touchy subject. In some areas, anchoring may be necessary due to fishing gear and other obstacles.

Going ashore or having a contagious disease would constitute a breaking of the rules. In other words, do not abuse the right. Do not make excuses that are not supportable.

If you are going to anchor you had best be well up on the attitude of the local authorities and the provisions of the Law of the Sea, see page 64 for details.

Other Definitions

AIS

Automatic Identification System. Transmits on VHF channels 87-B, 88-B, provides: position, speed, and other information about nearby vessels.

<http://www.navcen.uscg.gov/enav/ais/default.htm>

or

<http://tinyurl.com/3yhfg9>

Apostille

Double certification required by some countries where the country or state of document-issue, certifies the authenticity of the document signer.

<http://www.state.gov/m/a/auth/ >

or

<http://tinyurl.com/3aw6ce>

A good explanation can be found at this site.

<http://www.apostille.us/>

Certified Copy

Copies made and certified by the agency issuing the original document. Also copies certified by a Notary Public.

CFR

United States Code of Federal Regulations, see also U.S. Code Documents, page 45.

EEZ – Exclusive Economic Zone

Generally out to 200 miles.

<http://en.wikipedia.org/wiki/Exclusive_Economic_Zone>

or

<http://tinyurl.com/2whnb5>

NLR – Mass Market products are eligible for export with NLR (No License Required) to any end user (including government end users) in all countries except the seven (7) embargoed countries: Cuba, Iran, Iraq, Libya, North Korea, Sudan, and Syria. Mass Market products are eligible for de minimis treatment.

<http://www.esri.com/legal/export/export-definitions.html>

or

<http://tinyurl.com/2m3y3e>

Flag Country

The country to which a vessel is registered.

Foreign Built Vessel

Any vessel for which the ship's document specifies a shipyard outside the U.S. If the vessel's keel or hull was laid in a U.S. shipyard then it is entitled to be classified as U.S. built; be sure your ship's Document and paperwork reflects this fact. If there is any question about the vessel's build country hang onto the Builder's Certificate CG–1261.

Mutiny
Taking control of the vessel from the Master of the Vessel; by more than one person.

Proof of Duty
If you cannot find or have a copy or original of the duty paid for a *foreign* built vessel. Here are some steps that you can take that will *help*.

Have the boat examined by a Customs officer and have them certify a Customs Form 4457, Certificate of Registration for Personal Effects Taken Abroad. Fill out the form with the boat's information. This will prove that the boat is not being brought into the U.S. for the first time.

An alternate tactic is to have a certified copy of the *Abstract of Title*.

Any proof that you have that the boat was previously in the U.S. should help; receipts such as: fuel, repairs, moorage, a U.S. Customs Clearance form (see page 28) or Clearance Number. Clearance Numbers are recorded in your logbook, right?

State of Principle Use
Underway, moored, anchored, in the water, or tied to a dock; constitutes the place of *principle use*. On a trailer or ashore does not constitute "use". A dinghy carried on deck, or in davits, but not in the water is unlikely to be considered "use". Reciprocity is guaranteed by the Motor Boat Act (FSBA) of 1971 for a minimum of 60 days.

Voyage Data Recorder
A kind of "flight recorder" for large commercial vessels.

U.S. Code of Federal Regulations (CFR)

Most Recent U.S. CFR's
<http://www.access.gpo.gov/nara/cfr/cfr-table-search.html#page1>

or

<http://tinyurl.com/x9q7>

CFR 33 = Navigation & Navigable Waters (generally recreational regs).

CFR 46 = Shipping (generally commercial with some recreational regs).

USCG National Vessel Documentation Center
<http://www.uscg.mil/hq/g-m/vdoc/nvdc.htm >

or

<http://tinyurl.com/2kyzem>

FAQ

<http://www.uscg.mil/hq/gm/vdoc/faq.htm >

or

<http://tinyurl.com/2jjwx5>

Order Copies

Abstract of Title online or certified copies of the ship's Document:

https://vcart.velocitypayment.com/uscg/

or

<http://tinyurl.com/3afpow>

Early Renewal

The ship's document can be renewed (CG–1280) early, obtain the form from the website below, fax the form to: ☎ +1-304-271-2405

<http://www.uscg.mil/hq/gm/vdoc/forms/cg1280.pdf>

or

<http://tinyurl.com/2rqg8u>

Do not send the current document to the Coast Guard or surrender the original to anyone; it should always be aboard the vessel. If you need "real copies", get certified ones from the CG, see Order Copies

Certified copies of the ship's Document are available for $4 each, much preferable to questionable ones made on your copy machine.

<http://www.uscg.mil/hq/gm/vdoc/genpub.htm >

or

<http://tinyurl.com/2wowro>

Is the Vessel Tender Documented?

Documentation of your vessel does **not** cover the vessel's tender or dinghy, if they are motorized. These craft fall within the jurisdiction of the motorboat numbering laws of the state of principal use. Contact your state agency that handles the registration or numbering of motorboats for further information, see Numbering below.

<http://www.access.gpo.gov/nara/cfr/waisidx_07/46cfr67_07.html >

or

<http://tinyurl.com/3bu6ed>

Boat Name

If covered by the dinghy must be visible some other place on the mother vessel.

51

Numbered Vessels

A vessel that is numbered by the U.S. Coast Guard (currently all states do their own numbering) and any state that provides for it in their regulations, can allow a tender that is not separately numbered or registered.

At the option of each state, that the tender does not have an engine of more than 10 horsepower and that it is used solely to transport persons from that vessel directly to shore and *for no other purpose*. This is state dependent and if you operate with any powered dinghy out of state or in a foreign country, that it would be wise to register and number the dinghy-tender separately. [22]

Where the mother vessel is **numbered** and the tender is not being numbered separately, then the number for the tender consists of the numbered vessel's *Number* to which a space or "– " and has been added, and the number "1" or "2" in sequence, example: WA–1234–XX–1.

---

[22] CFR 46. Sec.173.13 Exemptions.

Documented Vessels

Where the tender is associated with a documented vessel, if the tender has a motor of any kind or size, then the tender has to be registered separately, no exceptions except lifeboats (tenders are not lifeboats).

You can confirm this by consulting a recent copy of Chapman Piloting & Seamanship.

Earthquakes

An earthquake that occurs while you are afloat is not liable to be noticeable unless you are in shallow water. John Rains reported that he experienced an earthquake while in Mexico; the boat was underway. The noise was like as if the boat had gone aground. There is a small but real possibility of a Tsunami occurring at the same time.

Port Royal, Jamaica was destroyed by an earthquake and subsequent Tsunami that occurred in the late 1600's. The ground liquefied, the buildings literally sank into the sand and the sea washed over the area to a height of 30 feet. The entire process was attributed to the *Wrath of God*, as Port Royal had the reputation as being the most degenerate place on earth. Pirate Captain Henry Morgan's coffin; reportedly floated up, out of the sand, and was swept out to sea.

Tsunami

If you are anchored in shallow water with a Tsunami approaching, your options are limited and require immediate attention. Being anchored is better than being swept into the shore, but not as desirable as being in deep water.

If you are sure that you can up-anchor and get to deep water, that is one thing. But, if you cannot get to deep water; remember that the speed of the water in shallow water, as it surges towards shore can easily exceed 20 knots. The average cruiser cannot reach such speeds and if attempted, to run against the surging water, would be swept back into the shore.

In general you are safer inside your boat and anchored, than outside and underway, if in shallow water.

Which brings up the definition of "shallow water". There is no simple number, that can be used to determine a safe water depth. Take it for granted that deeper is better; that 100 feet should be safe in many cases, but not all.

World Wide

Cruising Information

<http://asianyachting.com/default.htm>

<http://www.noonsite.com/>

Embassy Web Sites

– A –

AFGHANISTAN
http://www.embassyofafghanistan.org/

ALGERIA
http://www.algeria-us.org/

ANGOLA
http://www.angola.org/

ARMENIA
http://www.armeniaemb.org/

AUSTRALIA
http://www.usa.embassy.gov.au/

AUSTRIA
http://www.austria.org

AZERBAIJAN
http://www.azembassy.us/

– B –

BANGLADESH
http://www.bangladoot.org/

BAHRAIN
http://www.bahrainembassy.org/

BELARUS
http://www.belarusembassy.org/

BELGIUM
http://www.diplobel.us/

BELIZE
http://www.embassyofbelize.org/

BENIN
http://www.beninembassy.us/

BOLIVIA
http://www.boliviausa.org/

BOSNIA AND HERZEGO–VINA
http://www.bhembassy.org/

BOTSWANA
http://www.botswanaembassy.org/

BRAZIL
http://www.brasilemb.org/cultural/washington_events.shtml

BRUNEI
http://www.bruneiembassy.org/

BULGARIA
http://www.bulgariaembassy.org/

BURKINA
http://www.burkinaembassyusa.org/

BURUNDI
http://www.burundiembassyusa.org/

– C –

CAMBODIA
http://www.embassyofcambodia.org/

CAMEROON
http://www.ambacamusa.org/

CANADA
http://geo.international.gc.ca/canam/washington/menuen.asp

CHILE
http://www.chileusa.org/

CHINA

http://www.chinaembassy.org/eng/

COLOMBIA

http://www.colombiaemb.org/opencms/opencms/

COSTA RICA

http://www.costaricaembassy.org/

CROATIA

http://www.croatiaemb.org

CYPRUS

http://www.cyprusembassy.net/home/

CZECH REPUBLIC

http://www.mzv.cz/wwwo/?zu=washington

– D –

DENMARK

http://www.ambwashington.um.dk/en

DOMINICAN REPUBLIC

http://www.domrep.org/

– E –

ECUADOR

http://www.ecuador.org

EGYPT

http://www.egyptembassy.net/

EL SALVADOR

http://www.elsalvador.org/

ESTONIA

http://www.estemb.org/

ETHIOPIA

http://www.ethiopianembassy.org/index.shtml

– F –

FIJI

http://www.fijiembassydc.com/

FINLAND

http://www.finland.org/en/

FRANCE

http://www.ambafranceus.org/

– G –

GAMBIA

http://www.gambiaembassy.us/

GEORGIA

http://www.georgiaemb.org/

GERMANY

http://www.germany.info/relaunch/index.html

GHANA

http://www.ghanaembassy.org/

GREAT BRITAIN, UNITED KINGDOM OF

http://www.britainusa.com/

GREECE

http://www.greekembassy.org/Embassy/content/en/Root.aspx

GRENADA

http://www.grenadaembassyusa.org/

GUATEMALA

http://www.guatemalaembassy.org/main.php

GUINEA

http://guineaembassy.com/

GUYANA

http://www.guyana.org/govt/foreign_missions.html

– H –

HAITI

http://www.haiti.org/

HOLY SEE

http://www.holyseemission.org/

HONDURAS

http://www.hondurasemb.org/

HUNGARY

http://www.huembwas.org/

– I –

ICELAND

http://www.iceland.org/us

INDIA

http://www.indianembassy.org/newsite/default.asp

INDONESIA

http://www.embassyofindonesia.org/

IRAN

www.daftar.org

IRAQ

http://www.iraqiembassy.org/

IRELAND

http://www.irelandemb.org/

ISRAEL

http://www.israelemb.org/

ITALY

http://www.ambwashingtondc.esteri.it/ambasciata_washington

– J –

JAMAICA

http://www.jamaicanconsulatechicago.org/

JAPAN

http://www.embjapan.org/

JORDAN

http://www.jordanembassyus.org/new/index.shtml

– K –

KAZAKHSTAN

http://www.kazakhembus.com/

KENYA

http://www.kenyaembassy.com/

KOREA

http://www.koreaembassyusa.org/

KYRGYZ REPUBLIC

http://www.kyrgyzembassy.org/

– L –

LAOS

http://www.laoembassy.com/

LATVIA

http://www.latviausa.org/

LEBANON

http://www.lebanonembassyus.org/

LESOTHO

http://www.lesothoembusa.gov.ls/

LIBERIA

http://www.embassyofliberia.org/

LIECHTENSTEIN

http://www.liechtenstein.li/

LITHUANIA

http://www.ltembasyus.org/

LUXEMBOURG

http://www.luxembourgusa.org/

– M –

MACEDONIA

http://www.macedonianembassy.org/

MALI

http://www.maliembassy.us/

MARSHALL ISLANDS, REPUBLIC OF

http://www.rmiembassyus.org/

MEXICO

http://portal.sre.gob.mx/usa/

MICRONESIA

http://www.fsmembassydc.org/

MOLDOVA

http://www.embassyrm.org/

MONGOLIA

http://www.mongolianembassy.us/default.php

MOZAMBIQUE

http://www.embamoc-usa.org/

MYANMAR

http://www.mewashingtondc.com/

– N –

NAMIBIA

http://www.namibianembassyusa.org/

NEPAL

http://www.nepalembassyusa.org/

NETHERLANDS

http://www.netherlandembassy.org/homepage.asp

NEW ZEALAND

http://www.nzembassy.com/home.cfm?c=31&l=86&CFID=428854&CFTOKEN=39748729

NIGER

http://www.nigerembassyusa.org/

NIGERIA

http://www.nigeriaembassyusa.org/

NORWAY

http://www.norway.org/Embassy/embassy.htm

– P –

PALAU

http://www.palauembassy.com/

PANAMA

http://www.embassyofpanama.org/

PAPUA NEW GUINEA

http://www.pngembassy.org/

PERU

http://www.peruviannembassy.us/

PHILIPPINES

http://www.philippineembassyusa.org/

POLAND

http://www.polandembassy.org/

PORTUGAL

http://www.portugal.org/index.shtml

– Q –

QATAR

http://www.qatarembassy.net/

– R –

ROMANIA

http://www.roembus.org/

RUSSIA

http://www.russianembassy.org/

– S –

ST. VINCENT AND THE GRENADINES

http://www.embsvg.com/

SAUDI ARABIA

http://www.saudiembassy.net/

SIERRA LEONE

http://www.embassyofsierraleone.org/

57

SERBIA
http://www.yuembusa.org/

SINGAPORE
http://www.mfa.gov.sg/washington/

SLOVAK
http://www.slovakembassyus.org/

SOUTH AFRICA
http://www.saembassy.org

SPAIN
http://www.mae.es/Embajadas/Washington/en/Home/

SRI LANKA
http://www.slembassyusa.org/

SURINAME
http://www.surinameembassy.org/

SWEDEN
http://www.swedenabroad.se/pages/start_6989.asp

SWITZERLAND
http://www.swissemb.org

– T –

TAJIKISTAN
http://www.tjus.org/

TANZANIA
http://www.tanzaniaembassyus.org/

THAILAND
http://www.thaiembdc.org/index.htm

TUNISIA
http://tunisiaembassy.org/

TURKEY
http://www.turkishembassy.org/

TURKMENISTAN
http://www.turkmenistanembassy.org/

– U –

UGANDA
http://www.ugandaembassy.com/

UNITED ARAB EMIRATES
http://uaeembassy.org/

UKRAINE
http://www.mfa.gov.ua/usa/en/news/top.htm

URUGUAY
http://www.uruwashi.org/

UZBEKISTAN
http://www.uzbekistan.org/

– V –

VENEZUELA
http://www.embavenezus.org/

VIETNAM
http://www.vietnamembassyusa.org/

– Y –

YEMEN
http://www.yemenembassy.org/

– Z –

ZAMBIA
http://www.zambiaembassy.org/

EUROPEAN UNION
http://www.eurunion.org

The Language of Sailors

When a Loose Cannon Flogs a Dead Horse, There's the Devil to Pay: Seafaring Words in Everyday Speech. By Olivia A. Isil.

Plymouth Naval Sayings Page

<http://www.plymouth.gov.uk/homepage/leisureandtourism/libraries/whatsinyourlibrary/lns/navalsayings/navalsayingsac.htm>

or

<http://tinyurl.com/2wemcb>

U.S. State Tax Issues

Definition, Real versus Personal Property

Real Property is generally Real Estate; whereas, boats, planes and RV's are Personal Property.

Property Taxes

Personal property taxes on boats are local taxes, which means county and, or city. Boats may or may not be exempt from personal property taxes; by state, county or city. See page 65 for more detailed information:

<http://tinyurl.com/2w4tjd>

The table of Property Tax States where the table indicates: no tax. It means only in regards to *Recreational* Boats. For instance, Washington State taxes commercial boats. Where boats are not taxed, it is generally due to the notion that since they do not produce income, they are exempt, as in Texas.

There may be a few places where there is a property tax that is administered by some other government agency. Such a possibility cannot be absolutely excluded.

If you are a transient, being present in a marina on tax day, which is most likely January 1st, may get you entangled unnecessarily in the local tax system. In which case the safest bet is to be moored in a state that does *not* allow property tax on boats, or if they do, not in a county or city that does.

The tax due in such cases most likely consists of two parts, the county one and the city one. The city part is most likely a fraction of the county part. The valuation placed on the boat does not necessarily equal the market value; this is one more variable that is hard to pin down.

An example would be Edenton Marina, NC. Where you have to pay the annual city and county property tax, $56 county and $29 city per $10,000 valuation, i.e. for $100,000 property you pay $850.

You cannot rely on verbal or even written opinions, from state tax employees, or what is written here. In some states not even the opinions of local expert tax attorneys!

Maryland is the poster child for a state where you cannot rely upon any opinion except maybe the Judge who tries your case, maybe not the Judge.

The tables provided here cannot be relied upon as they contain unknown errors. Use it only as a rough guide to assist you in doing your own research.

There are numerous exemptions to the sales/use and property tax laws, some to your benefit and some not. There are complex exemptions for used boats.

None of this may apply to or should be relied upon at all if you are a resident of the state in question. In point of fact, this entire book is not intended as guidance for a resident of the state.

Do not respond to demands for information. Once you do, they then have added incentive to keep hounding you. Then you have created an implied obligation to continue to reply. Providing false information is a felony in many states, which is an added incentive not to reply.

If you get involved in property tax, you may also get hit for sales/use tax.

Some state tax employees have been reported to deliberately mislead in order to enhance tax revenue or fail to provide forms. In some cases the forms are now on the Internet.

There are basically three types of boat owners: those passing through, those trying to identify a suitable place to retire[23], or to moor somewhere distant from their place of residence. The material supplied here is targeted at those passing through.

Property taxes on city owned marinas: in some cases the tax is passed on as a separate bill, be sure to ask. Private marinas generally have the taxes built into the marina fee.

Under the exemptions topic is the issue of when the tax kicks in, by date, or minimum time. In some cases the tax is owed for vessels on site on Jan. 1 or whatever. In other cases it is depend-

---

[23] <http://www.retirementliving.com/RLtaxes.html>

ent on how many days you have been in the state.

There are probably exceptions to these generalizations. The only safe bet is to verify the situation in the target locale

Visit my web site page: <http://tinyurl.com/39lac6>

Instructions for locating current state/county/city tax rates.

Latest Sales Tax Rates, single page table

<http://www.taxadmin.org/FTA/rate/sales.html>

or

<http://tinyurl.com/pezxf>

Detail Information about State Taxes

<http://www.bankrate.com/brm/news/news_taxes_home.asp>

or

<http://tinyurl.com/yrv8bl>

This web site above is an excellent source of information; very comprehensive.

Definitions for State table

Consecutive

For instance, if a documented vessel from another state is brought into North Carolina for over 90 *consecutive* days, a decal must be purchased from North Carolina.

Registration w/Validation Decal

If the vessel is documented, *Yes* means the state requires a decal to be purchased and displayed after the reciprocity period expires. In some cases the state requires a decal *immediately,* if you do not have a current, in-force decal from some state; see Reciprocity Issues, page 34.

999 Days

Reciprocity means unlimited.

State by State

Registration Offices

Phone Numbers, Reciprocity, Decals

State	☎ Telephone	Reciprocity Days	Consecutive	Registration w/Validation Decal
Alabama	(334) 242-3673, #4	90	**	Yes, if used for pleasure
Alaska	(907)463-2297	90		No
Arizona	(602)942-3000	90		No
Arkansas	(501)223-6378	90		No
California	(916)657-8013	120		No
Colorado	(303)791-1954	60		No
Connecticut	(860)566-1556	60		Yes
Delaware	(302)739-3498	60	**	No
D.C., Washington.	(202)727-4582	180		Yes
Florida	(850)488-4676	90		Yes
Georgia	(770)414-3337	60	**	Yes
Hawaii	(808)587-1970	90		No
Idaho	(208)334-4180 x279	60	**	No
Illinois	(217)782-2138	60		Yes
Indiana	(317)233-5096	60	**	Yes
Iowa	(515)281-6579	60		Yes
Kansas	(316)672-5911 x127	60		No
Kentucky	(502)564-3074	999[24]	**	No
Louisiana	(504)765-2898	90		No
Maine	(207)287-5209	60		No
Maryland	(410)260-3220	30		Yes
Massachusetts	(617)727-3900	60	**	No
Michigan	(517)322-1460	60		Yes

[24] Not req'd if not perm resident

State	☎ Telephone	Reciprocity Days	Consec-utive	Registration w/Validation Decal
Minnesota	(612)296-2316	90	**	No
Mississippi	(601)432-2068	60		No
Missouri	(314)751-4509	60	**	Yes
Montana	(406)846-6000	90	**	No
Nebraska	(402)471-0641	60	**	No
Nevada	(775)688-1511	90		No
New Hampshire	(603)271-2333	30	**	Yes
New Jersey	(609)292-6500	180		Yes
New Mexico	(505)827-0612	999[25]		Yes
New York	(518)474-0445	90		Yes
North Carolina	(919)662-4373	90		NO, but can
North Dakota	(701)328-6300	180[26]		No
Ohio	(877)4-BOATERM	60	**	Yes
Oklahoma	(405)521-3221	60		Yes
Oregon	(503)373-1405 x254	60		Yes
Pennsylvania	(717)657-4551	60		Get valid decal, pay fee every 2 yrs.
Rhode Island	(401)222-6647	90		Yes
South Carolina	(803)762-5034	60	**	No
South Dakota	(605)773-3541	90		No
Tennessee	(615)781-6618	60	**	Yes
Texas	(800)262-8755	90	**	Yes
Utah	(801)297-750	14		Yes
Vermont	(802)828-2000	30[27]		Yes
Virginia	(804)367-1000	90		No

---

[25] Not req'd if not perm resident

[26] Req'd if primary use

[27] Valid. sticker 30-90, reg. after 90

State	☎ Telephone	Reciprocity Days	Consec-utive	Registration w/Validation Decal
Washington	(360)902-3770,#5	60. Then Apply 2x for 60 permit	**	No
West Virginia	(304)558-5351	60	**	No, but can
Wisconsin	(608)266-2141	60	**	Yes
Wyoming	(307)777-4683	90	**	No

Use Taxes

<http://tinyurl.com/2dw7pk>

Sales Taxes

<http://tinyurl.com/35alra>

Table of State Sales & Property Taxes for Boats

State & Contact	Sales Tax	Property Tax, Boats
Alabama Bill Garner, BLA, Marpol Dir.	2%	No
Alaska Jeff Johnson, BLA, Dept. of Natural Resources	None. Some boroughs with tax	No (State)
Arkansas Mike Wilson, BLA, Boating Safety Section	4.625%	Yes
Arizona Mark Weise, BLA, Game & Fish Dept.	8.1%	No
California Don Waltz, Chief of Boating Facilities Division	7.25%	Yes, local
Colorado Rick Storm, BLA, Div. of Parks & Outdoor Rec.	3%	No
Connecticut Eleanor Mariani, BLA, DEP: Boating Div.	6%	No. Higher reg. fee charged in lieu of taxes.
Delaware Chief Jim Graybeal, BLA; Div. of Fish & Wildlife	No sales tax	No
District of Columbia Lt. Alfred Durham, Metro Police Dept., Harbor Ptrl Sec.	None	No
Florida Sandra Porter, FFWCC, Div. of Admin. Services	6-7.5%	No
Georgia Lt. Col. Terry West, DNR, Wildlife Resources Div.	3.5% + local	Yes (county)

State & Contact	Sales Tax	Property Tax, Boats
Hawaii Mason Young, Boating Law Administrator, DLNR, Div. of Btg & Ocn. Rec.	None	Yes
Idaho Doug Strong, BLA; Dept. of Parks & Rec, Boating Program	5%	No
Illinois Greg Hunter, BLA; DNR, Office of Law Enforcement	7%	No
Indiana Sam Purvis, BLA; DNR, Law Enforcement Div.	5%	No. Excise tax coll. each yr based on new value of boat. Each yr tax is lwrd 10% down to 50% of orig. tax
Iowa Randy Edwards, BLA; DNR, Fish & Wildlife Div.	5%	No
Kansas Theri Swayne, BLA; KS Wildlife & Parks	4.9%	Yes
Kentucky Maj. Charles Browning, Dept. of Fish & Wildlife	6%	No
Louisiana Lt. Col Charles Clark, Dept. of Wldlf & Fisheries	8%	No
Massachusetts John Maxson, Dept. of Fisheries, Wildlife & Enviro. Law Enforcement	5%	No
Maryland Col. Doug DeLeaver, DNR, Natr'l Res. Police	5%	No. Excise Tax, one time.

State & Contact	Sales Tax	Property Tax, Boats
Maine Bill Swan, Dir. of Lic. & Reg., Dept. of Inlnd Fshrs & Wldlf	6%	Yes
Michigan Sgt. Henry Miazga, BLA; DNR, Law Enforcement Div.	6%	No
Minnesota Kim Elverum, BLA; DNR, Boat & Water Sfty. Coordinator	6.5% + .5% (in some cities)	No
Missouri Col. Jerry Adams BLA; Dept. of Publ. Safety, MO St. Water Patrol.	4.225%	Yes
Mississippi Maj. Kenny Neely, BLA; Dept. of Wildlife, Fisheries & Parks, Law Enforcement Div.	7%	Yes
Montana John Ramsey, BLA; MT Fish, Wildlife & Parks, Law Enforcement Div.	No sales tax	Yes
Nebraska Herb Angell, BLA; NE Game & Parks Cmsn, Outdoor Ed. Div.	4.5-6%	None
Nevada Fred Messman, BLA; Div. of Wildlife, Law Enforcement Div.	6.5% + local	Yes/ No; personal property tax incl in boat reg. fee
New Hampshire David T. Barrett, BLA; NH Dept. of Safety, Marine Patrol Div.	No sales tax	No
New Jersey Walter Schwatka, BLA; NJ State Police, Marine Services Unit	6%	Rec. boat. fee based on value of boat

State & Contact	Sales Tax	Property Tax, Boats
New Mexico Jerome Madrid, BLA, Enrgy, Mnrls & Natr'l Res, Btg Sfty Sec.	5%	No
New York Brian Kempf, BLA; Director, Bureau Marine & Rec. Vehicles	4% + local	No
North Carolina Capt. Mike Bogdanowicz NC Wildlife Resources – Enforcement	3%, up to $1500	Yes. 25 – 180/$10,000
North Dakota Nancy Boldt, BLA; Boat and Water Safety Coordinator	5% + local	No
Ohio Ken Alvey, BLA; DNR, Div. of Wtrcrft	5% + local	No
Oklahoma Lt. Bob Sanders, BLA; Dept. of Public Safety, Lake Patrol Div.	3.25%	No
Oregon Paul Donheffner, BLA; OR State Marine Board	No sales tax	No
Pennsylvania John Simmons, BLA; PA Fish & Boat Cmsn, Bureau of Btg. & Ed.	6%	No
Puerto Rico Ms. Marisa Gonzalez, BLA; Dept. of Enviro & Natr'l Res, Ofc of Cmsnr of Navigation	6.6% local sales tax	No
Rhode Island Steven Hall, BLA; Dept. of Enviro. Mgmt.	No sales tax on boats	No (except Westerly)
South Carolina Maj. Alvin Taylor, BLA; Tony Bates, Comptroller, DNR	6% up to $300	Yes $180/$10,000 appx.
South Dakota Bill Shattuck, BLA; Dept. Game, Fish & Parks, Div. of Wildlife	3% + local	No

State & Contact	Sales Tax	Property Tax, Boats
Tennessee Ed Carter, BLA; TN Wildlife Resource Agcy, Boating Div.	8.75%	No
Texas Dennis Johnston, BLA, Parks & Wldlf Dept., Law Enf. Div.	6.25	No
US Virgin Islands Lucia Roberts Francis, BLA; Dept. of Plng & Natr'l Res., Div. of Enviro Enf.	No sales tax on boats	No
Utah Ted Woolley, Boating Coordinator, Div. of Parks & Rec.	4.75% + local (1-2%)	Yes
Vermont Alan Buck, BLA; VT State Police, Marine Div.	5%	No
Virginia Charles Sledd, BLA; Dept. of Game & Inland Fisheries	5%	Yes, Not all Local Jurisdictions
Washington James Horan, BLA; Jim Eychaner, Intragcy Cmte for Otdr Rec.	7-8.6%	No, Recreational
Wisconsin John Lacenski, BLA; DNR, Div. of Law Enfrcmnt	5% + local	No
West Virginia Lt. Col. Bill Daniel, BLA; DNR, Law Enforcement Section	6%	Yes
Wyoming Russ Pollard, WY Game & Fish Dept.	4% + local	No

BLA means: Boating Law Administrator

Coastal Boat Property Tax States

State	Property Tax Averages: by State per $1000 of value	Tax per $100,000
Rhode Island[28]	16.72	$1672
Maine	13.03	$1303
Virginia	8.91	$891
Georgia	8.55	$855
North Carolina	7.63	$763
California	7.20	$720
Mississippi	6.18	$618
South Carolina	5.49	$549
Hawaii	3.08	$308

Explanation

The Property Tax numbers are averages for the entire state (2000). Are those intended for Real Estate (Property) and are provided only as a rough guide as to the likely tax on a Recreational boat in that state. The property tax is especially hard to swallow as it is generally a once a year tax, whereas sales and use taxes are one time; also excise taxes.

Property Tax States

AK, CA, GA, HI, IN, KS, ME, MO, MS, MT, NV, NC, SC, RI,

VA, WV

By Area

AK, CA, HI

ME, VA, WV, GA, MS, NC, SC, RI

IN, KS, MO, MT, NV.

---

[28] Town of Westerly, only.

By Highest Sales Tax

Then by highest Property Taxes

State & Contact	Sales Tax	Property Tax, Boats
Tennessee Ed Carter, BLA; TN Wildlife Resource Agcy, Boating Div.	8.75%	No
Washington James Horan, BLA; Jim Eychaner, Intragcy Cmte for Otdr Rec.	7-8.6%	No, Recreational
Arizona Mark Weise, BLA, Game & Fish Dept.	8.1%	No
Louisiana Lt. Col Charles Clark, Dept. of Wildlf & Fisheries	8%	No
Florida Sandra Porter, FFWCC, Div. of Admin. Services	6-7.5%	No
California Don Waltz, Chief of Boating Facilities Division	7.25%	Yes, local
Mississippi Maj. Kenny Neely, BLA; Dept. of Wildlife, Fisheries & Parks, Law Enforcement Div.	7%	Yes
Illinois Greg Hunter, BLA; DNR, Office of Law Enforcement	7%	No
Minnesota Kim Elverum, BLA; DNR, Boat & Water Sfty. Coordinator	6.5% + .5% (in some cities)	No
Utah Ted Woolley, Boating Coordinator, Div. of Parks & Rec.	4.75% + local (1-2%)	Yes
Puerto Rico Ms. Marisa Gonzalez, BLA; Dept. of Enviro & Natr'l Res, Ofc of Cmsnr of Navigation	6.6% local sales tax	No
Nevada Fred Messman, BLA; Div. of Wildlife, Law Enforcement Div.	6.5% + local	Yes/ No; personal property tax incl in boat reg. fee
Texas Dennis Johnston, BLA, Parks & Wildlf Dept., Law Enf. Div.	6.25	No
Maine Bill Swan, Dir. of Lic. & Reg., Dept. of Inlnd Fshrs & Wildlf	6%	Yes
West Virginia Lt. Col. Bill Daniel, BLA; DNR, Law Enforcement Section	6%	Yes

State & Contact	Sales Tax	Property Tax, Boats
Connecticut Eleanor Mariani, BLA, DEP: Boating Div.	6%	No. Higher reg. fee charged in lieu of taxes.
Kentucky Maj. Charles Browning, Dept. of Fish & Wildlife	6%	No
Michigan Sgt. Henry Miazga, BLA; DNR, Law Enforcement Div.	6%	No
New Jersey Walter Schwatka, BLA; NJ State Police, Marine Services Unit	6%	Rec. boat. fee based on value of boat
Pennsylvania John Simmons, BLA; PA Fish & Boat Cmsn, Bureau of Btg. & Ed.	6%	No
Nebraska Herb Angell, BLA; NE Game & Parks Cmsn, Outdoor Ed. Div.	4.5-6%	None
Virginia Charles Sledd, BLA; Dept. of Game & Inland Fisheries	5%	Yes, Not all locales
North Dakota Nancy Boldt, BLA; Boat and Water Safety Coordinator	5% + local	No
Ohio Ken Alvey, BLA; DNR, Div. of Wtrcrft	5% + local	No
Idaho Doug Strong, BLA; Dept. of Parks & Rec, Boating Program	5%	No
Indiana Sam Purvis, BLA; DNR, Law Enforcement Div.	5%	No. Excise tax coll. each yr based on new value of boat. Each yr tax is lwrd 10% down to 50% of orig. tax
Iowa Randy Edwards, BLA; DNR, Fish & Wildlife Div.	5%	No
Massachusetts John Maxson, Dept. of Fisheries, Wildlife & Enviro. Law Enforcement	5%	No
Maryland Col. Doug DeLeaver, DNR, Natr'l Res. Police	5%	No. Excise Tax One Time
Vermont Alan Buck, BLA; VT State Police, Marine Div.	5%	No
Wisconsin John Lacenski, BLA; DNR, Div. of Law Enfrcmnt	5% + local	No

State & Contact	Sales Tax	Property Tax, Boats
New Mexico Jerome Madrid, BLA, Enrgy, Mnrls & Natr'l Res, Btg Sfty Sec.	5%	No
Kansas Theri Swayne, BLA; KS Wildlife & Parks	4.9%	Yes
Arkansas Mike Wilson, BLA, Boating Safety Section	4.625%	Yes
Missouri Col. Jerry Adams BLA; Dept. of Publ. Safety, MO St. Water Patrol.	4.225%	Yes
Wyoming Russ Pollard, WY Game & Fish Dept.	4% + local	No
New York Brian Kempf, BLA; Director, Bureau Marine & Rec. Vehicles	4% + local	No
Georgia Lt. Col. Terry West, DNR, Wildlife Resources Div.	3.5% + local	Yes (county)
Oklahoma Lt. Bob Sanders, BLA; Dept. of Public Safety, Lake Patrol Div.	3.25%	No
Colorado Rick Storm, BLA, Div. of Parks & Outdoor Rec.	3%	No
South Dakota Bill Shattuck, BLA; Dept. Game, Fish & Parks, Div. of Wildlife	3% + local	No
North Carolina Capt. Mike Bogdanowicz NC Wildlife Resources – Enforcement	3%, up to $1500	Yes. 25 – 180/$10,000[29]
South Carolina Maj. Alvin Taylor, BLA; Tony Bates, Comptroller, DNR	6% up to $300	Yes[30] $180/$10,000 appx.
Alabama Bill Garner, BLA, Marpol Dir.	2%	No
Hawaii Mason Young, Boating Law Administrator, DLNR, Div. of Btg & Ocn. Rec.	None	Yes
Montana John Ramsey, BLA; MT Fish, Wildlife & Parks, Law Enforcement Div.	No sales tax	Yes
Rhode Island Steven Hall, BLA; Dept. of Enviro. Mgmt.	No sales tax on boats	No (exc. Westerly)

---

[29] <http://tinyurl.com/3axl9o>

[30] <http://tinyurl.com/35oayo>

State & Contact	Sales Tax	Property Tax, Boats
US Virgin Islands Lucia Roberts Francis, BLA; Dept. of Plng & Natr'l Res., Div. of Enviro Enf.	No sales tax on boats	No
Alaska Jeff Johnson, BLA, Dept. of Natural Resources	None/Some boroughs w/tax	No (State)
Delaware Chief Jim Graybeal, BLA; Div. of Fish & Wildlife	No sales tax	No
District of Columbia Lt. Alfred Durham, Metro Police Dept., Harbor Ptrl Sec.	None	No
New Hampshire David T. Barrett, BLA; NH Dept. of Safety, Marine Patrol Div.	No sales tax	No
Oregon Paul Donheffner, BLA; OR State Marine Board	No sales tax	No

The Politics of Property Taxes on Boats

Boat costs go up faster than housing.

Boats generally depreciate, homes generally the opposite.

Boat values are harder to determine, due to custom building and lack of similar sales to use as guidelines.

The bigger and more expensive the boat, the more incentive to move the boat where it will not be taxed. High property taxes drive boats away.

Legally avoiding the tax is easy enough, that the gain in taxes often many times less than the loss of general business acquired from the boat's presence.

Connecticut dropped, its property tax on boats in 1981 and replaced it with a simple excise tax, collected at registration time; much less costly to administer.

Innocent Passage – UN Law of the Sea

Part 2 Territorial Sea, Sections 3 and Section 4 – Contiguous Zone

Part 3 – Straits

Part 4 – Archipelagic

Only the material from Part 2, Section 3 is included here. Part 2, Section 4 pertains to material for the Contiguous Zone; the material pertaining to Straits and Archipelagic States I have not included as it is nearly identical.

Part II
TERRITORIAL SEA AND CONTIGUOUS ZONE

SECTION 3. INNOCENT PASSAGE IN THE TERRITORIAL SEA

SUBSECTION A. RULES APPLICABLE TO ALL SHIPS

Article 17

Right of innocent passage

Subject to this Convention, ships of all States, whether coastal or land-locked, enjoy the right of innocent passage through the territorial sea.

Article 18

Meaning of passage

1. Passage means navigation through the territorial sea for the purpose of:

(a) traversing that sea without entering internal waters or calling at a roadstead or port facility outside internal waters; or

(b) proceeding to or from internal waters or a call at such roadstead or port facility.

2. Passage shall be continuous and expeditious. However, passage includes stopping and anchoring, but only in so far as the same are incidental to ordinary navigation or are rendered necessary by *force majeure* or distress or for the purpose of rendering assistance to persons, ships or aircraft in danger or distress.

Article 19

Meaning of innocent passage

1. Passage is innocent so long as it is not prejudicial to the peace, good order or security of the coastal State. Such passage shall take place in conformity with this Convention and with other rules of international law.

2. Passage of a foreign ship shall be considered to be prejudicial to the peace, good order or security of the coastal

State if in the territorial sea it engages in any of the following activities:

any threat or use of force against the sovereignty, territorial integrity or political independence of the coastal State, or in any other manner in violation of the principles of international law embodied in the Charter of the United Nations;

any exercise or practice with weapons of any kind;

any act aimed at collecting information to the prejudice of the defense or security of the coastal State;

any act of propaganda aimed at affecting the defense or security of the coastal State;

(e) the launching, landing or taking on board of any aircraft;

(f) the launching, landing or taking on board of any military device;

(g) the loading or unloading of any commodity, currency or person contrary to the customs, fiscal, immigration or sanitary laws and regulations of the coastal State;

(h) any act of willful and serious pollution contrary to this Convention;

(i) any fishing activities;

(j) the carrying out of research or survey activities;

(k) any act aimed at interfering with any systems of communication or any other facilities or installations of the coastal State;

(l) any other activity not having a direct bearing on passage.

Article 20

Submarines and other underwater vehicles

In the territorial sea, submarines and other underwater vehicles are required to navigate on the surface and to show their flag.

Article 21

Laws and regulations of the coastal State relating to innocent passage

1. The coastal State may adopt laws and regulations, in conformity with the provisions of this Convention and other rules of international law, relating to innocent passage through the territorial sea, in respect of all or any of the following:

(a) the safety of navigation and the regulation of maritime traffic;

(b) the protection of navigational aids and facilities and other facilities or installations;

(c) the protection of cables and pipelines;

(d) the conservation of the living resources of the sea;

(e) the prevention of infringement of the fisheries laws and regulations of the coastal State;

(f) the preservation of the environment of the coastal State and the prevention, reduction and control of pollution thereof;

(g) marine scientific research and hydrographic surveys;

(h) the prevention of infringement of the customs, fiscal, immigration or sanitary laws and regulations of the coastal State.

2. Such laws and regulations shall not apply to the design, construction, manning or equipment of foreign ships unless they are giving effect to generally accepted international rules or standards.

3. The coastal State shall give due publicity to all such laws and regulations.

4. Foreign ships exercising the right of innocent passage through the territorial sea shall comply with all such laws and regulations and all generally accepted international regulations relating to the prevention of collisions at sea.

Article 22

Sea lanes and traffic separation schemes in the territorial sea

1. The coastal State may, where necessary having regard to the safety of navigation, require foreign ships exercising the right of innocent passage through its territorial sea to use such sea lanes and traffic separation schemes as it may designate or prescribe for the regulation of the passage of ships.

2. In particular, tankers, nuclear-powered ships and ships carrying nuclear or other inherently dangerous or noxious substances or materials may be required to confine their passage to such sea lanes.

3. In the designation of sea lanes and the prescription of traffic separation schemes under this article, the coastal State shall take into account:

(a) the recommendations of the competent international organization;

(b) any channels customarily used for international navigation;

(c) the special characteristics of particular ships and channels; and

(d) the density of traffic.

4. The coastal State shall clearly indicate such sea lanes and traffic separation schemes on charts to which due publicity shall be given.

Article 23

Foreign nuclear-powered ships and ships carrying nuclear

or other inherently dangerous or noxious substances

Foreign nuclear-powered ships and ships carrying nuclear or other inherently dangerous or noxious substances shall, when exercising the right of innocent passage through the territorial sea, carry documents and observe special precautionary measures established for such ships by international agreements.

Article 24

Duties of the coastal State

1. The coastal State shall not hamper the innocent passage of foreign ships through the territorial sea except in accordance with this Convention.

In particular, in the application of this Convention or of any laws or regulations adopted in conformity with this Convention, the coastal State shall not:

(a) impose requirements on foreign ships which have the practical effect of denying or impairing the right of innocent passage; or

(b) discriminate in form or in fact against the ships of any State or against ships carrying cargoes to, from or on behalf of any State.

2. The coastal State shall give appropriate publicity to any danger to navigation, of which it has knowledge, within its territorial sea.

Article 25

Rights of protection of the coastal State

1. The coastal State may take the necessary steps in its territorial sea to prevent passage which is not innocent.

2. In the case of ships proceeding to internal waters or a call at a port facility outside internal waters, the coastal State also has the right to take the necessary steps to prevent any breach of the conditions to which admission of those

ships to internal waters or such a call is subject.

3. The coastal State may, without discrimination in form or in fact among foreign ships, suspend temporarily in specified areas of its territorial sea the innocent passage of foreign ships if such suspension is essential for the protection of its security, including weapons exercises. Such suspension shall take effect only after having been duly published.

Article 26

Charges which may be levied upon foreign ships

1. No charge may be levied upon foreign ships by reason only of their passage through the territorial sea.

2. Charges may be levied upon a foreign ship passing through the territorial sea as payment only for specific services rendered to the ship. These charges shall be levied without discrimination.

SUBSECTION B. RULES APPLICABLE TO

MERCHANT SHIPS AND GOVERNMENT SHIPS

OPERATED FOR COMMERCIAL PURPOSES

Article 27

Criminal jurisdiction on board a foreign ship

1. The criminal jurisdiction of the coastal State should not be exercised on board a foreign ship passing through the territorial sea to arrest any person or to conduct any investigation in connection with any crime committed on board the ship during its passage, save only in the following cases:

(a) if the consequences of the crime extend to the coastal State;

(b) if the crime is of a kind to disturb the peace of the country or the good order of the territorial sea;

(c) if the assistance of the local authorities has been requested by the master of the ship or by a diplomatic agent or consular officer of the flag State; or

(d) if such measures are necessary for the suppression of illicit traffic in narcotic drugs or psychotropic substances.

2. The above provisions do not affect the right of the coastal State to take any steps authorized by its laws for the purpose of an arrest or investigation on board a foreign ship passing through the ter-

ritorial sea after leaving internal waters.

3. In the cases provided for in paragraphs 1 and 2, the coastal State shall, if the master so requests, notify a diplomatic agent or consular officer of the flag State before taking any steps, and shall facilitate contact between such agent or officer and the ship's crew. In cases of emergency this notification may be communicated while the measures are being taken.

4. In considering whether or in what manner an arrest should be made, the local authorities shall have due regard to the interests of navigation.

5. Except as provided in Part XII or with respect to violations of laws and regulations adopted in accordance with Part V, the coastal State may not take any steps on board a foreign ship passing through the territorial sea to arrest any person or to conduct any investigation in connection with any crime committed before the ship entered the territorial sea, if the ship, proceeding from a foreign port, is only passing through the territorial sea without entering internal waters.

Article 28

Civil jurisdiction in relation to foreign ships

1. The coastal State should not stop or divert a foreign ship passing through the territorial sea for the purpose of exercising civil jurisdiction in relation to a person on board the ship.

2. The coastal State may not levy execution against or arrest the ship for the purpose of any civil proceedings, save only in respect of obligations or liabilities assumed or incurred by the ship itself in the course or for the purpose of its voyage through the waters of the coastal State.

3. Paragraph 2 is without prejudice to the right of the coastal State, in accordance with its laws, to levy execution against or to arrest, for the purpose of any civil proceedings, a foreign ship lying in the territorial sea, or passing through the territorial sea after leaving internal waters.

Territorial, Contiguous & EEZ Claims

In Nautical Miles

Country [31]	Territorial Sea	Contiguous Zone
Albania	12	
Algeria	12	24
Angola	12	24
Antigua and Barbuda	12	24
Argentina	12	24
Australia	12 [32]	24
Bahamas	12	
Bahrain	12	
Bangladesh	12	18
Barbados	12	
Belgium	12	24
Belize	12 [33]	

---

[31] Wikipedia <http://en.wikipedia.org/wiki/Territorial_waters>

[32] Australia: The territorial sea boundaries between the islands of Aubusi, Boigu and Moimi and Papua New Guinea and the islands of Dauan, Kaumag and Saibai and Papua New Guinea, together with such other portion of the outer limit of the territorial sea of Saibai are determined by a treaty with Papua New Guinea. The territorial seas of the islands known as Anchor Cay, Aubusi Island, Black Rocks, Boigu Island, Bramble Cay, Dauan Island, Deliverance Island, East Cay, Kaumag Island, Kerr Islet, Moimi Island, Pearce Cay, Saibai Island, Turnagain Island and Turu Cay do not extend beyond 3 nautical miles from the baselines.

[33] Belize: 3 nautical miles limit applies from the mouth of Sarstoon River to Ranguana Caye.

Country [31]	Territorial Sea	Contiguous Zone
Benin	200	
Brazil	12	24
Brunei	12	
Bulgaria	12	24
Cambodia	12	24
Cameroon	12 [34]	
Canada	12	24
Cape Verde	12	24
Chile	12	24
People's Republic of China	12	24
Republic of China	12	
Colombia	12	
Comoros	12	
Congo	200	
Cook Islands	12	
Costa Rica	12	
Cote d'Ivoire	12	
Croatia	12	
Cuba	12	24
Cyprus	12	24
Democratic People's Republic of Korea	12	50 [35]

---

[34] Cameroon: See article 45 of Law 96-06 of 18 January 1996 on the revision of the Constitution of 2 June 1972.

[35] 50-nautical-mile (93 km) military zone. Army Command Announcement of 1 August 1977..

Country [31]	Territorial Sea	Contiguous Zone
Democratic Republic of the Congo	12	
Denmark	12 [36]	
Djibouti	12	24
Dominica	12	24
Dominican Republic	6	24
Ecuador	200 [37]	
Egypt	12	24
El Salvador	200	
Equatorial Guinea	12	
Eritrea	12	
Estonia	12 [38]	
Fiji	12	
Finland	12 [39]	14

Country [31]	Territorial Sea	Contiguous Zone
France	12	24
Gabon	12	24
Gambia	12	18
Georgia	12	
Germany	12	
Ghana	12	24
Greece	6 [40]	
Grenada	12	
Guatemala	12	
Guinea	12	
Guinea-Bissau	12	
Guyana	12	
Haiti	12	24
Honduras	12	24
Iceland	12	
India	12 [41]	24
Indonesia	12	
Iran	12	24
Iraq	12	
Ireland	12	
Israel	12	
Italy	12	
Jamaica	12	24

[36] Denmark: Act No. 200 of 7 April 1999 on the delimitation of the territorial sea does not apply to the Faroe Islands and Greenland but may become effective by Royal Decree for those parts of the Kingdom of Denmark with the amendments dictated by the special conditions prevailing in the Faroe Islands and Greenland. As far as Greenland is concerned, the outer limit of the external territorial waters may be measured at a distance shorter than 12 nautical miles from the baselines.

[37] Ecuador: The 200 nautical miles limit is in effect only between the continental territorial sea of Ecuador and its insular territorial sea around the Galápagos Islands.

[38] Estonia: In some parts of the Gulf of Finland, defined by coordinates.

[39] Finland: Extends, with certain exceptions, to 12 nautical miles, unless defined by geographical coordinates. In the Gulf of Finland, the outer limit of the territorial sea shall at no place be closer to the midline than 3 nautical miles, according to the Act amending the Act on the Limits of the Territorial Waters of Finland (981/95).

[40] Greece: 10-nautical-mile (18.5 km) limit applies for the purpose of regulating civil aviation.

[41] India: 12 nautical mile limit includes Andaman, Nicobar and Lakshadweep.

Country [31]	Territorial Sea	Contiguous Zone	Country [31]	Territorial Sea	Contiguous Zone
Japan	12 [42]	24	Nicaragua	12	24
Jordan	3		Nigeria	12	
Kenya	12		Niue	12	
Kiribati	12		Norway	12	24
Kuwait	12		Oman	12	24
Latvia	12		Pakistan	12	24
Lebanon	12		Palau	3	
Liberia	200		Panama	12	24
Libya	12		Papua New Guinea	12 [44]	
Lithuania	12		Peru	200 [45]	
Madagascar	12	24	Philippines	[46]	
Malaysia	12		Poland	12	
Maldives	12	24	Portugal	12	24
Malta	12	24	Qatar	12	24
Marshall Islands	12	24	Republic of Korea	12	24
Mauritania	12	24	Romania	12	24
Mauritius	12		Russia	12	24
Mexico	12	24	Saint Kitts and Nevis	12	24
Micronesia	12				
Monaco	12				
Morocco	12	24			
Mozambique	12	24			
Myanmar	12	24			
Namibia	12	24			
Nauru	12	24			
Netherlands	12				
New Zealand	12 [43]	24			

[42] Japan: 3 nautical mile limit applies to the Soya Strait, the Tsugaru Strait, the eastern and western channels of the Korea Strait and the Osumi Straits only.

[43] New Zealand: 12 nautical mile limit includes Tokelau.

[44] Papua New Guinea: 3 nautical miles in certain areas.

[45] Peru: The 200 nautical mile territorial sea is called 'Maritime Dominion' in article 54 of the 1993 Constitution: " ...In its maritime dominion, Peru exercises sovereignty and jurisdiction, without prejudice to the freedoms of international communication, in accordance with the law and the treaties ratified by the State..."

[46] Philippines (Rectangle defined by coordinates. Claim extends beyond 12 nautical miles).

Country [31]	Territorial Sea	Contiguous Zone
Saint Lucia	12	24
Saint Vincent and the Grenadines	12	24
Samoa	12	24
São Tomé and Príncipe	12	
Singapore	3	
Saudi Arabia	12	18
Senegal	12	24
Seychelles	12	24
Sierra Leone	12	24
Slovenia	[47]	
Solomon Islands	12	
Somalia	200	
South Africa	12	24
Spain	12	24
Sri Lanka	12	24
Syria	12	24
Sudan	12	18
Suriname	12	
Sweden	12	
Syria	12	
Thailand	12	
Timor-Leste	12	
Togo	30	
Tonga	12	

Country [31]	Territorial Sea	Contiguous Zone
Thailand	12	24
Timor East	12	24
Trinidad & Tobago	12	24
Tunisia	12	24
Turkey	6 [48]	
Tuvalu	12	24
Ukraine	12	
United Arab Emirates	12	
United Kingdom	12 [49]	
United Republic of Tanzania	12	
United States of America	12	24
Uruguay	12	24
Vanuatu	12	24
Venezuela	12	15
Vietnam	12	24
Yemen	12	24

Contiguous Zones where there is no cell entry means that the country has no declared contiguous zone.

---

[47] Slovenia (DLM means that "the national legislation establishes the limits of a given zone only by reference to the delimitation of maritime boundaries with adjacent or opposite States, or to a median (equidistant) line in the absence of a maritime boundary delimitation agreement")

[48] Turkey: 6 nautical miles in the Aegean Sea, 12 nautical miles in the Black Sea.

[49] United Kingdom: Also 3 nautical miles. (3 nautical miles in Anguilla, Guernsey, British Indian Ocean Territory, British Virgin Islands, Gibraltar, Monserrat and Pitcairn; 12 nautical miles in United Kingdom, Jersey, Bermuda, Cayman Islands, Falkland Islands, Isle of Man, Saint Helena and Dependencies, South Georgia, South Sandwich Islands, and Turks and Caicos Islands.)

Bibliography

General

A Captain's Guide to: Transiting the Panama Canal in a Small Vessel, by David W. Wilson. 1999

Chapman Piloting & Seamanship ISBN 158816232X

Farwell's Rules of the Nautical Road. Craig H. Allen.

Offshore Sailing: 200 Essential Passagemaking Tips. By Bill Seifert.

The Voyagers Handbook. Beth Leonard.

Merchant Marine Officers' Handbook. 5th Ed.

Recommended Reading List

New Zealand Mariners Handbook. Ed. Tim Ridge

Empire of Blue Water. Stephan Talty. Captain Morgan's Great Pirate Army.

Dennis L. Noble. Lifeboat Sailors: Inside the Coast Guard's Small Boat Stations. Washington, D.C.: Brassey's, 2000.

Dennis L. Noble. The Rescue of the Gale Runner: Death, Heroism, and the U.S. Coast Guard. Gainesville: University Press of Florida, 2002.

Dennis Noble. Rescued By the U.S. Coast Guard: Great Acts of Heroism Since 1878. Annapolis: Naval Institute Press, 2004.

Advanced Sailing. Tony Gibbs.

Outfitting. Practical Sailor.

Yachtsman's Emergency Handbook. N. Hollander.

The Ocean Sailing Yacht. Donald Street.

Blue Water Cruising. Bob & Nancy Griffith.

Understanding Rigs and Rigging. Richard Henderson.

Sea Sense. Richard Henderson.

Cruising Routes. Jimmy Cornell.

Voyaging under Power. Beebe & Lieshman.

The Merck Manual. (Medical).

Heavy Weather Sailing. Adlard Coles.

50 Things You Must Know Before You Travel to Mexico. James Truette

<http://tinyurl.com/29ths8>

Cruising As A Way Of Life. Thomas Colvin.

The Boat Repair Manual. Buchanon.

Metal Boats. Bruce Roberts-Goodson.

Steel Away – A Guidebook to the World of Steel Sailboats. Smith & Moir

<http://www.windroseaway.com/steelaway.html>

Steel Boatbuilding : From Plans to Launching. Thomas Colvin.

Boatbuilding with Steel, Gilbert C. Klingel.

Boatbuilding with Aluminum, Stephen F. Pollard.

Cambium Woodworking Web Site.
<http://www.cambiumbooks.com/books/boat_building/>

Understanding Yacht Design. Ted Brewer

Sailing Yacht Designs. Bob Perry

The Desirable and Undesirable Characteristics of Offshore Yachts. John Rousmaniere.

Lonely Planet, series of travel books. Go to the travel guides section.

<http://www.lonelyplanet.com/>

Safety Recommendations for Cruising Sailboats.

<http://www.ussailing.org/merchandise/detail.asp?product_id=51025>

Practical Sailor – Tips, Tools & Techniques

<http://www.practicalsailor.com/tools/features.html>

Liveaboard Magazine

<http://www.livingaboard.com/>

or

<http://tinyurl.com/2tp7lp>

Smuggling in the Old Days.

Smuggling in Cornwall. <http://www.connexions.co.uk/culture/smuggler.htm>

Smuggling & Shipwrecks. <http://www.bl.uk/learning/langlit/texts/ship/shipwrecksandsmuggling.html>

King's Cutters – the Revenue Service and the War Against Smuggling

Outlaws of the Lakes: Bootlegging & Smuggling from Colonial Times to Prohibition

Sea Wolves And Bandits

Tales of the Cornish Smugglers

The Scottish Smuggler

The Pirates Lafitte

Night Landing: A Short History of West Coast Smuggling: Heron, David

The Pirate Hunter, The True Story of Captain Kidd, By Richard Zacks

A sample of a rare book advertisement[50] for:

SMUGGLING IN CORNWALL BY FRANK GRAHAM

A Son of Australia. Memories of W.E. Parry-Okeden, ISO, 1840–1926

Brisbane, Watson, Ferguson, 1928. Octavo, xiv, 342 pages plus 19 plates. Gilt-decorated cloth; top edge lightly foxed; endpapers offset; essentially a very fine copy. At fourteen, Parry-Okeden was 'one of a Volunteer Force formed to assist in dealing with the trouble which culminated in the Ballarat riots'; after ten years of pastoral experience in Queensland, in 1870 he 'accepted the task of organizing, training, and leading' the Border Patrol, formed to put an end to smuggling along the southern and south-western borders of that colony; from 1895 to 1905, he was Commissioner of Police in Queensland. **$350**

---

50 <http://www.treloars.com/catalogues/r99.htm>

INDEX

A

Alameda, 19, 22
Anchoring, 48, 75

B

bootleg, 1

C

Certified Copy, 27
Clearance Number, 5, 50
COLREGS, 2

E

Exempt, 3, 8, 9, 10, 30, 35, 38, 52

F

fine, 15, 30
fined, x, 2, 9, 13, 15
fines, 3, 5, 11
Foreign, i, ix, 1, 10, 22, 36, 37, 38, 42, 47, 49

I

innocent, 26, 48
Innocent, 24, 47, 48, 75
Internet, x, 37, 41

N

notice, 11, 15, 45
Notice, 3, 11, 12, 44, 45

P

Pilotage, 37, 38
Portsmouth, 19, 22
Proof of Duty Paid, 27

R

Reciprocity, 34, 36, 50, 61
Registration, 1, 4, 10, 23, 27, 28, 34, 35, 36, 37, 39, 46, 50, 51
Rescue, 19, 21, 22, 23, 85

S

Salvage, 19, 90, 91, 92, 93
Sojourners, 37

T

Tax, 35, 37
Taxes, x, 1, 35, 36, 37

U

US Coast Guard, xi, 19, 21, 22, 51
US Customs, xi, 5, 6, 8, 30, 31, 43, 50
US State Department, 19

V

Visa, 6, 33

W

Web, xi, 6, 37

Forthcoming Books from Capt. Mike

See author's web site:

<http://www.yachtsdelivered.com/bookpub.html>

Salvage

Remember that you have a copy of the salvage form here in your "emergency kit", along with emergency numbers. Better to rip up this book, than to be without a Salvage Form, if you need one.

U.S. Coast Guard Emergency Numbers, see page 19

BoatUS Salvage

<http://www.boatus.com/towing/guide/salvage/contract.asp>

or

<http://tinyurl.com/36sygn>

PDF version

<http://www.boatus.com/salvage/contract.pdf>

or

<http://tinyurl.com/2kkdsq>

Salvage Form

Page 1 of 3, STANDARD FORM YACHT SALVAGE CONTRACT

Boat Owners Association of The United States

STANDARD FORM YACHT SALVAGE CONTRACT

It is hereby agreed this _____ day of _____, 20___,

at _____ hours at _____ (location)

by and between:_____

    (Owner or Captain)

for the Yacht named "_____,"

which is described as a ("Vessel") _____

    (yr – manufacturer – length)

and insured by: _____ ("Underwriter")

and _____, (Salvage Company/Salvor)

to salvage the yacht under these terms and conditions:

1. Salvor agrees to render assistance to and endeavor to save said yacht and its property and deliver her afloat or ashore at _____ marina or port as mutually agreed, or to nearest safe port if unspecified herein, as soon as practicable.

2. Salvor shall have the requisite possession and control of the subject yacht and be entitled without expense to the reasonable use of the yacht and its gear in the performance of recovery or salvage operations.

3. Said salvage and any towage services by the Salvor shall terminate upon delivery of said yacht as designated herein. Owner and Underwriter shall be responsible for any storage, towing or other port or marina charges following delivery and for risk of loss thereafter.

(a) NO CURE/NO PAY (Compensation, including special compensation, to be determined under ARTICLES 13 and 14, SALCON 89, and U.S. Admiralty Law.)

INITIALS _____/_____ salvor/owner

(b) NO CURE/NO PAY, AT A FIXED PRICE of $_____

INITIALS _____/_____ salvor owner

(c) NO CURE/NO PAY at $_____/per hour/per day/per vessel (or in accordance with SALVOR's published rates, initialed and attached hereto).

INITIALS _____/_____ salvor /owner

(d) OTHER:

Page 2 of 3, STANDARD FORM YACHT SALVAGE CONTRACT

4. Compensation to Salvor for the services performed hereunder shall be in accordance with a billing and any supportive analysis of the salvage operation to be presented to Owner and underwriter's agents upon completion of salvage. Billing to be calculated on the basis specified in No. 3. No agreement on price or its reasonableness has been made at the scene unless agreed to in writing.

5. Services hereunder are rendered on a "No Cure, No Pay" basis; however, salvor shall be entitled to a reasonable allowance for prevention or minimization of environmental damage in accordance with Articles 13 & 14 of the 1989 International Convention on Salvage, as well as for clean up or wreck removal in the event the vessel is deemed a constructive total loss. Payment is due promptly upon presentation of Salvor's bill. Interest at the rate of one and one-half (1.5%) percent per month (or the maximum legal rate allowed) shall accrue on any unpaid balance from 30 days after completion of salvage and presentation if a salvage bill, or as determined in accordance with the findings of any Arbitration Award.

6. In the event of any dispute regarding this salvage or concerning the reasonableness of any fees or charges due hereunder, all parties agree to binding local arbitration utilizing individual(s) experienced in maritime and salvage law. The Boat Owners Association of The United States Salvage Arbitration Plan, though not required, is available as a public service through Boat Owners Association of The United States wherever the parties agree to its use. In the event Owner is uninsured for payment of these services, Salvor may, at its election, agree with Owner to use any agreeable arbitration system or to proceed with all available legal remedies to recover sums believed due and owing.

7. It is understood that services performed hereunder are governed by the Admiralty and Maritime Jurisdiction of the Federal Courts and create a maritime lien against the yacht or its posted security. Salvor's lien shall be preserved until payment. Salvor agrees in lieu of arrest or attachment to accept from the yacht's Underwriter, a Letter of Undertaking for an amount equal to one and one-half (1.5) times the presented billing with a copy of the insurance policy and coverage information. If the yacht is uninsured or its Underwriter cannot provide a Letter of Undertaking, Salvor may demand the posting of a Surety Bond with its designated Escrow Agent in an amount equal to 1.5 times the Salvor's bill. Salvor may satisfy collection of fees or charges hereunder by recourse to any security posted and shall be entitled to any costs incurred in collection of payments due hereunder including reasonable attorneys fees subject to the findings of any arbitration.

8. Salvor hereby warrants that it is acting on its own behalf and on behalf of any subcontractors retained by Salvor to perform services in the recovery or delivery of the yacht. Salvor shall be responsible for any such subcontractors' compensation.

9. In the event the Salvor has already rendered salvage services to the described yacht prior to execution of this contract, the provisions of this contract shall apply to such salvage services.

Page 3 of 3, STANDARD FORM YACHT SALVAGE CONTRACT

SIGNED:_____
Owner/Captain or Owner's Agent

SIGNED:_____
Salvage Company

Owner Print Name & Address: _____
_____
_____

Phone: (___) _____ Fax: (___) _____

Salvor Print Name & Address: _____
_____
_____

Phone: (___) _____ Fax: (___) _____

www.ingramcontent.com/pod-product-compliance
Lightning Source LLC
LaVergne TN
LVHW022112080426
835511LV00007B/766